color your home beautiful

Ideas and Solutions

color your home beautiful

Ideas and Solutions

THUNDER BAY
P·R·E·S·S

San Diego, California

Thunder Bay Press

An imprint of the Advantage Publishers Group

5880 Oberlin Drive, San Diego, CA 92121-4794

www.advantagebooksonline.com

All notations of errors or omissions should be addressed to Thunder Bay Press, editorial department, at the above address. All other correspondence (author inquiries, permissions) concerning the content of this book should be addressed to Rockport Publishers, Inc., 33 Commercial Street, Gloucester, Massachusetts 01930-5089. Telephone: (978) 283-9590; Fax: (978) 283-2742 www.rockpub.com

ISBN 1-57145-847-6

Library of Congress Cataloging-in-Publication Data available upon request.

Grateful acknowledgment is given to Anna Kasabian for her contribution to pages 66-67, 70-75, 100-101, 104-107, 132-139, 152-153, 156-159, 184-191, 216-217, 220-223, 260-261, and 264-295; to Martha Gill for her contribution to pages 60-65, 76-99, 108-131, 140-151, 160-183, 192-215, and 224-259; and to Mark McCauley for his contribution to pages 12-57, 68-69, 102-103, 154-155, 218-219, 262-263, and 296-302.

Cover Image: Winfried Heinz/Living, Etc/IPC Syndication (top left);
            Huntley Hedworth/Red Cover (top right);
            Mark York/Red Cover (bottom left);
            Kevin Thomas (bottom right)

Printed in China
1 2 3 4 5 02 03 04 05 06

contents

COLOR FUNCTIONS AND COLOR THERAPY 9

    Colors for Serenity 10

    Colors for Healing 18

    Colors for Clarity 32

    Colors for Nurturing 38

    Colors for Spirituality 44

CHOOSING THE RIGHT COLORS FOR YOU 57

    Primarily Red 64

    Spicy 74

    Exotic 86

    Essentially Orange 98

    Dynamic 106

    Natural 118

    Primarily Yellow 130

    Luminescent 138

    Essentially Green 150

    Tropical 158

    Tranquil 170

    Primarily Blue 182

    Coastal 190

    Classic 202

    Essentially Violet 214

    Icy 222

    Luxurious 234

    Romantic 246

    Simply Neutral 258

MOOD—WITH COLOR 278

THE COLOR-CHOICE QUIZ 294

BIBLIOGRAPHY 301

DIRECTORY OF PHOTOGRAPHERS AND DESIGNERS 302

ABOUT THE AUTHORS 304

color functions
and color therapy

COLORS FOR SERENITY

SERENITY IS ESSENTIAL IN THESE RUSH-HERE, RUSH-HOUR-THERE LIVES OF OURS.

WE ALL SEARCH FOR PEACE IN OUR TIME, WHICH SOMETIMES SEEMS IMPOSSIBLE

IN A DYNAMIC AND CONSTANTLY CHANGING WORLD. TO INCREASE OUR SENSE OF

THE SERENE, WE CREATE PLACES OF CONTEMPLATION WITHIN THE HOME. IN ORDER

TO DESIGN A SERENE, RELAXING ENVIRONMENT WITH COLOR, IT IS NECESSARY TO

LOOK AT ALL THE ELEMENTS THAT GO INTO A ROOM. BY CHOOSING THE PROPER

COLOR PALETTE, YOU CAN DESIGN AN ENVIRONMENT IN WHICH TO RELAX AND

REFLECT—THE HOME AS REFUGE, AS THE SAYING GOES. MEDITATE ON THAT!

opposite: Orange walls delineated with white trim provide this bathroom with the feeling of sunset. The orange glow of the sun is translated into wall color relating to the end of day and a time for recovery, peaceful and alone with one's thoughts.

Analogous colors, colors located next to each other on the color wheel, produce serenity. To create an ambiance of tranquil understanding, combine turquoise with analogue blue, which provides aspects of truth and stability to the eternal nature of turquoise, representing clarity of thought. Medium red with orange yields an environment long on inner power with a foundation of earthiness. Try a combination of neutral tones, such as beiges with chocolate browns, to convey brown's feeling of comfort with the blending capabilities of beige. Deep or medium grays bring a sense of solid stone. Use with silent black and heavenly white to produce inner strength. Add a single bright red rose to the room to focus your moments of meditation.

Look to colors that have calming qualities in their darker values, such as blue, green, purple, brown, or gray for the dominant hue in the serene space. Accents can bring any number of secondary emotions to the room; choose red to signify the heart, medium intensities of pink for a sense of innocence, violet for friendship, or gold for permanence.

To accentuate the sacred aspects of a space, use dark purple with gold, which brings quietude with the dark value of purple while providing a feeling of the eternal with rich gold as the secondary hue. A third color can also be used to enhance the space. Green plants placed about

BRING THE OUTSIDE IN

Any interior environment is an attempt to replicate the outside world. Decorate your rooms in terms of color value just as the exterior environment is arranged, with darker values below (the earth), medium values as you move upward in a space (trees, hills, and mountains), and lighter values at ceiling height (sky). It's your world, and welcome to it!

left: This is a welcoming sight after a hard day at work. Serenity as a form of escape is found here. Browns and beiges combine to reduce stress through analogous combinations.

the room, as the healer, or black accents, such as wrought iron, impart a sense of the past. While away the hours on a trip through time with royalty and luxury calming the senses.

Similarly toned colors in dark, middle, or light ranges also effect a calming interior. Blue married with terra-cotta shades of orange is grounding, representative of the totality of earth and sky. Winter whites with light blues create a silent winterscape. Green with analogous yellow is relaxing and summery, while deeper shades of orange with brown give a sense of long evenings surrounded by silent fall colors.

When medium to dark orange is used as the largest color in a space, its sublime power and representation of the earth will produce a serene effect. Partner this with verdant, medium greens and bark browns as counterpoints to give the room a calm coolness that recalls the restfulness of a stand of trees at sunset. To complete the scene, use faded beige as an accent color in decorative objects that have a tumbled-stone quality, bringing the outdoors in and creating your own indoor garden getaway.

Green always helps promote relaxation. Dark green walls add a forestlike quietude and seclusion to a room. Use a medium beige color for the trim to define the edges of your arboretum. Add rough saddle-leather upholstery to suggest ruggedness, orange for casual comfort, or accents regal red to promote formality and family ties.

above: Heaven in a wild flower, eternity in an hour. This forever flower, imitating the forever sun, blooms blessed in the brazen colors of the day, orange and yellow. It thus sends sunshine back to the sun. It's infinity at your feet.

opposite: Serenity is achieved here through the use of alternating vertical stripes that enclose the environment with an overall sense of stability and protection, even though the coloration is lively. Deep values of pink are sedating.

HEALING HEALING HEALING HEALING HEALING

COLORS FOR HEALING

COLOR HAS BEEN USED AS HEALER SINCE TIME IMMEMORIAL. WHEN TAKEN

IN LARGE DOSES OR SMALL, HEALING HUES ARE THE SHAMAN OF THE SENSES,

REENERGIZING THE WEARY AND CALMING THE ANXIOUS. WHEN INGESTED BY THE

VIEWER, THESE COLORS CAN PROMOTE A HEALTHIER, HAPPIER LIFE. SIMPLY

SURROUNDING YOURSELF WITH LIFE-AFFIRMING COLOR CHANGES YOUR THINK-

ING AND PROVIDES SOMETIMES SUBTLE, SOMETIMES DRAMATIC CHANGE.

HOWEVER IT IS USED, COLOR IS A TOOL FOR FIXING WHAT AILS US. THE DOCTOR IS

IN, IN A COAT OF MANY COLORS.

above: Healing red relates to the blood that flows through us all. Note how the darker values on the right in the upholstery fabric pull your attention to the right side of the frame first.

First among the healers of the color wheel is green. Green is nature's visual muscle relaxant. In dominant hue, either light valued or dark, green assuages. Use it in its dark ranges as a thematic color to calm, or in lighter values to revitalize. Marry green wall color to analogous blue upholstery to create a liquidity of motion and a semblance of ease. In combination with yellow, it serves up refreshing vistas, healing through the suggestion of the lazy days of summer and the newness of spring.

Red is the color of the blood that courses through our veins. In this sense, the color is reassuring and constant, reminding the viewer of healthy existence, and has been long held as a symbol of well-being. Red is the glow of the fire that fuels our imaginations and provides for meditative thought. We stare endlessly into red flames and feel calmed and warm. And, of course, red is love, and knowing that we are loved always makes the heart pump faster. The space defined by red speaks of sensuality and touch, massaging our cares with *amore*. Relax in a red

left: Red, white, and pink heal through the suggestion of purity represented by the white day-bed and the *joie de vivre* of pink.

opposite: A pervasive sense of health and well-being is conveyed by the womblike atmosphere shown here.

above: Green soap brings the healing power of green to clean. And cleanliness is next to godliness, which we would assume is a good thing. So wash up! Physician, heal thyself with green.

opposite: Communication of our inner worlds is represented by lilac with brilliant white, giving a heavenlike appearance to the space. Soul mates talk to one another, alone together.

leather chair to be reminded of tradition and the balm of brandy on a cold winter's night. Red combined with green tells of high holidays, of being surrounded by the healing power of family and dear friends.

White is the epitome of health. In representing cleanliness, it shortens the time we feel pain. White sheets beckon us to lie down and free ourselves from the hurt of movement and the aches of long days. White walls calm the senses through the very lack of distracting color. White distills the environment, washing the space in whiteness and removing harmful elements, and, in so doing, erasing our worries as well. When combined with blue walls, white upholstery is refreshing breaths of fresh air, cloudlike in feel. White linen tablecloths stimulate the sense of taste by removing potentially clashing colorations from the scene. Partner white with turquoise to suggest clear thinking and feelings of health.

TESTING YOUR COLORS

Be sure to take a look at fabric and paint swatches in the environment in which they will be placed. View the color at different times of day, paying close attention to the color during the time you are most in the space. For example, look at the swatch under artificial light at night, if that is primarily when you use the room.

Purple is associated with the mind and emotion. This color impacts our mental health, especially when incorporated with healing green. A space with light values of purple is mentally invigorating, clearing up the miasma caused by the very dynamism of life. When yellow serves as secondary color to purple, attentiveness elevates; with green, mental acuity is slowed. Purple is the emotional healer; it serves to penetrate to the source of psychic pain and bring curative power to those suffering from inner hurt.

bottom: White suggests a healthy lack of distracting color. We all need a break from the perception of color, at times. White relieves the eye and gives us a shot at visual recovery.

opposite: Health-giving green with lilac relates to the slowing down of mental acuity, just in time for a quick siesta. The room is active in coloration, yet softer values are used to denote peace. Each color represents a different aspect of the space. Note the use of complementary color on the wall trim.

following page, left: Overall, black is healing, as in the placidity of the starry night.

following page, right: Summer clouds surround the chef. The airiness of the blue wall is enhanced by the whiteness of the cabinet.

Brown is often used on upholstery in casual scenarios such as family rooms—a welcome retreat after a hard day. Beige induces healthful sleep, providing respite in its unchallenging nature and curing with its restorative qualities. Incorporated with brown, the protective feeling of analogous closeness envelopes us in folds of comfort. Bedrooms casually dressed with the protective nature of brown for wall color as cuddle-up bed coverings hasten dreamy sleep. Color is the medicine we take when we're in need. So take your medicine; it's the color-doctor's orders.

FORMALITY VS. INFORMALITY

Complementary color schemes are more formal in feeling than analogous schemes, which tend to be more restful. Use complementary schemes (red/green or blue/yellow) in medium to light values in the formal areas of the home, such as the living room or dining room. Save analogous schemes for family rooms and bedrooms, where respite is desired.

above: Healing is found in unassuming beige. This bedroom lulls us to sleep with beige as unchallenging somnambulist.

opposite: Beige softens the contemporary line of the sofa, while the silvery gray pillow is used as a counter. Note the sense of primitive fantasy in the clay accent pieces on the mantel.

When your thoughts race and your heart pounds, blue soothes. The color acts as a grounding force in our lives, enhancing meditative skills. Blue is the sedative of the senses. Other more numinous attributes of the heavenly hue bring blue out of the realm of the purely physical and into the mystic of the metaphysical.

Blue expands our sensitivity to the needs of others and our ability to get in touch with our own feelings. The nonverbal cues that we pick up from blue include those of tradition and that of belonging to a group. Blue conveys this sense of safety within the confines of the group and thereby increases our sense of worth and value as contributors to society. We are the Blue Man Group.

above: Lavish lilac colors the walls, relating to our internal psyches, while beige sets the stage for the healing power of inner peace found in this room. Stable blue on the throw pillow with blonde wood tables continue the similarly valued story, increasing the lighter-than-air feeling of floating in space. Transcendental healing takes place in rooms such as this.

opposite: Dark values of blue call out to comfort us. We are drawn to the dark-valued bed, wanting to stretch out and close our eyes for just a few minutes. Note the comfortable chocolate brown, which adds to the serenity of the space.

CLARITY CLARITY CLARIITY CLARITY

COLORS FOR CLARITY

USE COLOR TO HEIGHTEN CLEAR THINKING AND FURTHER YOUR INTELLECTUAL

PURSUITS. CLEARLY DEFINE EACH INDIVIDUAL ELEMENT IN THE ROOM, GIVING IT A

SPECIFIC PLACE OF ITS OWN, BY COMBINING DIFFERENT HUES WITH NEUTRALS

SUCH AS PURE WHITE OR BEIGE. THIS CREATES AN ENVIRONMENT THAT IS CON-

DUCIVE TO SKILL AND CRAFT, THE WORK OF OUR HANDS AND MINDS AND, THUS,

OUR HEARTS. GOD IS IN THE DETAILS, AND THE DETAILS ARE MULTIHUED.

ACHIEVE CLARITY WITH COMPLEMENTARY, AS OPPOSED TO ANALOGOUS,

SCHEMES. THESE COLORS, OPPOSITES ON THE COLOR WHEEL, ALWAYS CREATE A

DISTINCT DIVISION OF COLOR WHEN THEY ARE PAIRED. INCORPORATE VARYING

VALUES OF COMPLEMENTARY COLORS IN A ROOM TO HEIGHTEN PERCEPTION, AS

THE TONAL CONTRASTS ARE IMMEDIATELY NOTICEABLE.

opposite: Orange-finished kitchen cabinetry is clearly apart from the dining area, done up in black and white. Note how colors are moved from one space to another, thereby providing a unifying effect. Metallic silver is pulled from the wall splash in the kitchen into chairs and the table base.

Light tones on dark grounds are delineated from their surroundings. They send messages that there are functional differences between the shapes found in a room, such as a white mantel standing highly defined against a red wall. This sense of clarity is important to use as a definer of space, whether active or passive. Complementary color schemes are more formal in feeling, while the opposite is achieved when using analogous colors that fade into each other.

Black with white is the essence of opposites, providing a no-nonsense atmosphere. The absence or addition of light (which black and white represent) relieves the eye of the burden of color definition, freeing us to search out more lofty goals. Clinical in nature, white, when used in toned-down values as a wall color, eases eye strain, while black serves as counterpoint, clearly stating line. Large squares of black and white tile have long been identified as traditional flooring; zebra 'stripes add a dash of black/white animal sensitivity to any room. The formal black sofa

above: The white towel is obviously separated from the overall blue tone of the space.

opposite: Note how the darker floor, medium wall values, and lighter ceiling delineate each area of the space, as in the exterior environment: dark-valued earth, medium values as seen in trees, and lighter sky above.

leaps from the white-defined interior, while white faux fur on the floor is art deco chic. Black, white, and gray have also made the transition to contemporary styles in the products of the post modern; the kitchen with stainless steel appliances and black granite countertops surrounded by white cabinetry speaks volumes about serious cooks.

When looking for clarity, look particularly to spring, which is captured in colors that bring the season of renewal indoors. Use sprays of flowers, whether in natural bunches or formally arranged, to freshen your interiors. Light values are always springlike. Yellows, pinks, and lavenders create a visual impact and also remind us of the fresh scent of spring. To soften a room and make it more feminine and wistful, use saffron as a wall color, pink bed coverings, and white lace window treatments. Hotter intensities convey the vitality of the season and can dress up the lowly spare bedroom with shots of soft color.

Orange is a clarion call to the senses. Transcendent in nature, orange creativity is the warm glow of inner knowledge. Clearly cutting through the clutter, orange hops to attention and regales the senses.

above: Clearly the plant is not part of the vase, though the stem color is replicated by the transparent green. Springlike in feel, the scene recalls the yellow of the sun, found in the tabletop; green symbolizes living things in the vase form; and pink is related to the season of renewal.

NURTURING NURTURING NURTURING NURTURING NURTURING NURTURING

COLORS FOR NURTURING

NURTURING IS ALL ABOUT LOVE: LOVE OF OURSELVES AND OUR NEAREST AND DEAREST. IN THIS LOVE WE SHOW CARING, WE COMFORT, WE TENDERLY SEE TO THE NECESSARY ASPECTS OF LIVING. LIKEWISE, SUSTAINING OURSELVES IS OF PREEMINENT IMPORTANCE, FOR WITHOUT IT WE OBVIOUSLY CAN'T GO ON. WE MUST CARE FOR OUR PHYSICAL BODIES, FEEDING, PROVIDING WATER, CLEANSING, AND RESTING. SEEING TO OUR EMOTIONAL WELL-BEING IS ALSO PARAMOUNT IN ORDER TO LEAD A FULL LIFE. ENHANCE THESE PROCESSES BY USING COLOR'S ASSOCIATIONS AND STIMULATIONS. HAVE YOU HUGGED YOUR INTERIOR DESIGN TODAY? HAS YOUR INTERIOR DESIGN HUGGED YOU?

above: Nurture your cares away. Daily stresses need to be relieved. The inviting bath in hard white porcelain is softened by the deep pink above the wainscotted lower wall. Tender coloration relates to our inner child.

STAGES OF LIFE

Think about who will be using a room before you decide on color. Relate the colors you choose to the ages of the inhabitants. Soft pastels keep an infant's environment soothing, while primaries in their brazen brightness are often used to invigorate the older generations.

Nurturing others is a corollary of the maternal instinct and is a significant factor in our lives as social beings. Environments colored in dedication to our emotional selves activate certain feelings that we would like to encourage, while also elevating the nurturing sides of our personalities. Red relates to love, purple addresses inner peace, and blue represents security.

right: The color of the sky lassoed and brought to earth in wall color. This room belies any possible staleness with blue transferring the outdoors in. And, as fresh air tends to make one feel drowsy, the room creates its own!

COLOR AND ARCHITECTURE

If you live in a style of home that has historical reference, study the colors that are associated with that particular style. Medium to dark greens are popular in arts and crafts style; a particular shade of medium blue is associated with federal style while deep red is seen as an important element of Victoriana.

left: Red, seen here with a white border, relates to the appetite and is often used in restaurants to stimulate our desire for nourishment. The atmosphere is inviting and clearly defined for dining.

COLORS FOR SPIRITUALITY

OUR LIVES ARE NOT CONFINED TO THE MERELY PHYSICAL. WERE THIS SO, LIFE

WOULD BE EMPTY, DEVOID OF MEANING. FOR MILLIONS THE WORLD OVER, FEEDING

THE SOUL IS A DAILY EXERCISE. IN MANY CULTURES (AND IN MANY PREVIOUS ERAS),

ALLOCATING A SPACE THAT ALLOWS FOR PRAYERFUL THOUGHT IS A NECESSITY

OF LIFE. CREATING IN ITSELF IS AN ACT OF SPIRITUALITY, AND IN DECORATING THE

SACRED SPACE WE PRAY TWICE, MUCH AS THOREAU WARMED HIMSELF TWICE

FIRST BY CHOPPING WOOD, THEN BY BURNING IT.

A SPIRITUAL ENVIRONMENT INCLUDES COLORS THAT RADIATE SUBLIME

QUIETUDE OR ARE HEAVY WITH SYMBOLISM. FOR THE ROOM'S DOMINANT HUE,

CHOOSE MEDIUM TO DARKER VALUES THAT GIVE CALMNESS AND SERENITY, SUCH

AS BROWN OR BLUE. IN MANY FAITHS, CERTAIN COLORS ARE A SHORTHAND FOR

opposite: Alive with the power of the almighty sun and the purple raiment of Menelaus, it's a pagan delight! Worship Apollo or find your own Muse; either way the room is ready for a journey through the past in electric hues suggestive of regality and high intellectual concepts while wed in dynamic complementary fashion.

spiritual communion; orange traditionally suggests the radiation of inner spirit, forest green is contemplative, and red signifies the heart. Colors such as these free your thoughts to meditate on the infinite and start or end your day connected to a higher power.

Perhaps the most obvious spiritual color is white. White has a purifying effect on an environment when it is used in large quantities on walls or represented on special spiritual occasions in decorative objects. White, as the innocence of love, creates a feeling of oneness with the spiritual world. Use symbolic colors as contrast in a white-walled environment to lend a sense of emotional clarity to a room. High contrast will make inspirational objects leap from the surroundings and into the consciousness. For a feeling of the

top: Pure white cleanses the soul as well as the body. When used with healing green, the sense of spiritual healing is increased.

opposite: Calming blue soothes the soul in cool tile and wall color. Lie back in the drawn bath and let blue canoe you to a spiritual realm.

opposite: The star of Bethlehem has fallen to earth. Float on white clouds through blue nocturne to the houses of the holy.

bottom: The glow of inner knowledge is represented by the clay wall. This is counterpointed with eighteenth-century Rationalism as evidenced in the Hepplewhite-style chairs in gray. John Wesley could methodically cook-up Methodism here.

right: The Romanesque arches on the wall in faux stone finish are reminiscent of early Christian churches. The overall room color combined with the serenity of the bath sedates the mind and the body while cleansing the soul. Note the "Shepard's Crook" motif, an early symbolic Christian metaphor, on the window treatments.

COLOR AND SPACE

The colors you choose will have an impact on the perceived size of your room. Darker shades will seem to make a space contract, while light values make a room expand. Don't fall into the trap of always using color to expand a small space. Try going with the architectural nature of the room, and instead use dark colors to increase the sense of cozy closeness.

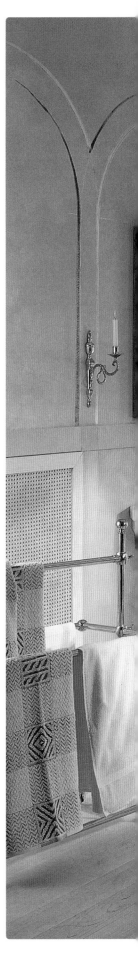

following page, left: The Buddha statue begninly oversees the moonswept colors here. The serenity of the Oriental garden at evening, with bathtub as a reflecting pool, brings Siddhartha to your home.

following page, right: These medieval musings are for the Gothic aficionado. The black of the wrought iron as an accent against the casually styled orange window treatments brings to mind the all-perasive spirituality of the Middle Ages. One expects to hear Gregorian chants echo through the space.

USE LIGHT FOR IMPACT

The light source itself will affect your colors. Florescent light tends toward the blue range, while incandescent light is yellowish. Fluorescents in the kitchen make the hard-surfaced space harder and flattens out colors. Incandescent bulbs are warmer, tending to better highlight colorations.

accents such as wrought iron impart a sense of the past. Black also offers dignified strength and simultaneously suggests both the earth-bound and the limitless universe. Gray is the color of rock, serene in its appearance of solidity. The gray-themed space ties us to tradition, to ancient holy places hewn from stone. Beige can relate to the serenity and spiritual escape of the monk's cell through its unassuming nature.

Lighter values bring happiness, suggesting a world filled with eternal love and peace. These colors create calmness during times of high stress. They bring us hope in the light green of early spring, joy in bright yellow, and innocence in youthful pink. Green is the elysian fields, the color of easy living, far from the worries of winter. The yellow room is alive with the light of a power

greater than ourselves. Pink is our child-like wonder before things boundless and eternal, reminding us that we are perpetually seeking guidance and knowledge. Lilac represents intuition, filling us with a sense of peaceful knowing.

Finally, color is a tool we use to nurture and heal. These two processes are closely associated with the divine, especially when intertwined with creation. Utilizing color to enhance our spiritual well-being is a necessary and inescapable fact of life. We run to it and it answers our prayers, bringing us to life eternal through deep symbolic meaning and by focusing our faith in meditative moments. It reminds us of what life really means and helps us tired travelers find haven. Color is the safe harbor for the ships of our souls.

choosing the right colors for you

To make it as easy as possible to choose colors and select palettes for your home, the following section is divided into color and mood sections. Choose the atmosphere that you'd like to create in your home, then select from the thirty-six color combinations featured within that color mood. In each mood, large swatches of colors reflect classic combinations, as well as the latest trends, such as cool, synthetic ice tints; warm, rich chocolate and mocha coffee hues; deep lemon yellows and tangy citrus oranges; translucent blues; sun-bleached wood tones; and deep indigos.

Decorating tips show you how to choose and use color in your home, including valuable advice on selecting fabrics, paint, furniture, and accessories to create the look you want.

Explore each color and mood to discover your intuitive color sense. Hundreds of modern color combinations for the new century are packed within these pages, ranging from adventurous palettes that motivate to classic design principles freshly paired with color inspiration. For example, learn how a well-planned palette can soften a minimal design, enrich a classic interior, or gently enhance a natural composition. Discover how an organic shape can complement an earthy palette, or how fabric selection can create a mood that generates excitement. Find out how light, texture, fabric, proportion, shape, and scale work together to contribute to the color focus and ambiance of a room.

Historical and cultural influences continue to have a dominant presence within the world of decoration and design. Trends include revivals of vintage blends, such as the pastels and autumnal colors of the 1950s; the reinvention of the 1960s' psychedelics; an overhaul of the 1970s' earth tones; and synthetic futuristic hues. Interiors are influenced not only by past decades, but also by lifestyle. Holistic living has created an interest in cool, stress-relieving interiors for the home inspired by health spa environments. Ecological concerns have led to an unprecedented demand for environmentally friendly materials, such as jute, hemp, and canvas. The popularity of second homes has opened up the opportunity for playful design. Lively and amusing decor, once the province of youth, is now sought by the young at heart.

Although color choices have never been so widely available, expansive, or exciting for the professional and home designer, selecting multiple colors to develop palettes need not be daunting or even complicated. Use this book to make sense out of the avalanche of color options and to guide you in selecting colors that express your style. With this book as your guide, you can build beautiful palettes to transform your home with color.

Reading the color formulas:

#'s correspond with colors reading from outside to inside

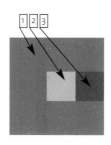
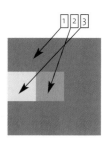

Some people like red but tend to shy away from it in their décor because it's a big color and makes what they feel is too strong a statement. If you'd like to use red, but don't want to overwhelm your space with it, consider introducing it in a way that will bring out the qualities you admire. Take a step back and think about how you can take the color and gently weave it into your roomscapes.

The Red Range
The great thing about red is that its range is very dramatic, which gives you many opportunities to use it in different rooms and create distinctly different moods. Deep, dark, rusty red can create the perfect warmth for a library or establish an elegant mood in a dining room. On the other end of the red spectrum, the palest of pinks combined with moss green and yellow can be the perfect backdrop for an ultra-feminine dressing room. Introduce tomato red with bright yellow accents to a kitchen, and even on the dreariest winter day, you'll feel energized.

Bringing Red Into the Scene
Think about the level of red you want to introduce in your home. It can come in many forms, and you can easily turn the volume of red up or down. Here are a few of the ways to bring on the red:

• Upholstery: For a splash of red, one red velvet chair; for more, an entire red couch. Choose a pattern with other colors, and work off that as your palette.

• Wall coverings: As an accent, choose one red for one wall and create a scene that shows off an elegant table and glass vase. For a bigger statement, paint an entire room fire engine red and weave in deep, dark blues and crisp whites with furnishings.

• Window treatments: Drama comes through loud and clear if you paint your walls linen white and frame your windows in an apple red. Accessorize with rugs that blend rich red tones with warm hues or cool, depending on the mood you want.

• Art: Use red to subtly jazz up a low–key décor with art–whether it's a glass collection in shades of red or paintings with red as the main color.

• Floor covering: Work with red only in your rugs, and build a palette from the ground up. The warmth and drama can build up and around the room.

Red Combinations
On the color wheel, red moves from rich, spicy hues all the way to pale, dreamy pink tones. Consider these combinations:
• Red and green
• Three consecutive hues or tints of red
• Red and blue
• Red in a variety of tints

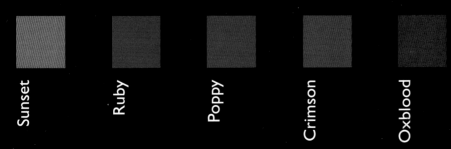

Sunset   Ruby   Poppy   Crimson   Oxblood

Don't want to paint your walls red? How about the ceiling? This windowless corridor glows in a cocoon of ruby-red and gold and leads the way to a light-filled room in a similar palette. Notice how the lamps, little red box, and art splashed with red combine to complete a look.

When red takes the lead, it makes a statement about you and how you like to live. This elegant living room shows how red to the max can pull together a fresh, dramatic look, all the while holding onto a bit of tradition.

SUSAN MOORE,
A MINNESOTA-BASED COLORIST:

"Everyone thinks the wall with art should be white. I have 56 pieces of art with color behind it. I think when you have, for example, a painting with a lot of red in it and you put it against a green wall, it becomes important; you create a focal point.... I find a lot of people who like red [and] use it as the color they don't have in their lives; they use it to motivate themselves. They're usually introverts! I told some-one who said they wanted more courage to do something that they should buy some red underwear! Red is about bravery and courage."

NEW YORK— AND BOSTON-BASED INTERIOR
DESIGNER CELESTE COOPER:

"In one project, the client specifically asked for red. And here I used it on lacquered walls in the dining room, picked it up as an accent on seating in the kitchen, [and added it in] a leather insert in the floor, handrails in the foyer, and on little tables in the living room. In this case, the most important issues were balance and repetition."

**NEW YORK—BASED INTERIOR DESIGNER
LEE BOGART:**

"I use red a lot, a real tomato red. It's a wonderful color choice when you don't have a lot of architectural detail. When you walk into a red room it makes a wonderful statement. To me it's a neutral because you can use it with brown, blue, pink, and yellow tones."

**CHRIS CASSON MADDEN, A NEW YORK—
BASED DESIGN EXPERT, AUTHOR AND
FURNITURE DESIGNER:**

"I have to admit that 18 years ago I did paint an old pine library red, and took steel wool and glazed over it. It glows in the dark! When people hear I've had a red room in my life they can't believe it...but I needed that secret red room. Now we're loosening up about color, and loving it."

**KAKI HOCKERSMITH, INTERIOR DESIGNER
FOR THE WHITE HOUSE UNDER THE
CLINTON ADMINISTRATION:**

"I think red, one of my favorite colors, is the most challenging to work with.... I might go through four or five paint sample books before I find the right one because there aren't that many good choices."

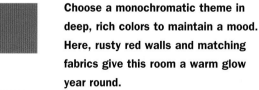

Choose a monochromatic theme in deep, rich colors to maintain a mood. Here, rusty red walls and matching fabrics give this room a warm glow year round.

If you want to show off your art, set it on a deep-colored background. In this eclectic room, each piece of art and each element of the various collections stands out—perhaps just what the owner wanted!

 A collection of red pillows in different color combinations provides the perfect dash of color and drama to an all-white room. This color strategy frees you to experiment with color with little financial commitment.

Talk to a paint expert about bringing texture to your walls with different painting techniques. Here, the red-brown walls have been sponge-painted in a swirling pattern that accentuates the rich palette. Notice, too, how the art, frames, rug, and fabrics share earthy tones, and how each stands on its own against the wall of color.

PARIS-BASED INTERIOR DESIGNER SYLVIE NEGRE:

"In the North of Paris we have a lot of 'silver days,' so in sophisticated flats I will prefer to use a lot of darkish red. It helps to warm it up. Then, on a wall, you can have yellow or terra cotta, or a large stripe with white, green, and red, or even material from old French fabrics..."

BARBARA MAYER, NEW YORK–BASED AUTHOR, LECTURER, BENJAMIN MOORE ARCHIVE CONSULTANT:

"My kitchen is an example of a color scheme I've had for over 20 years. It's Chinese red on the top cabinets, and the inside is painted sunny yellow. Every time I open those cabinets I get a great deal of pleasure. In fact, it was the kitchen cabinets that made me decide to get more color in other rooms."

JEAN TOWNSEND, PROFESSIONAL PAINTER AND CO-OWNER OF DROLL DESIGN:

"I always seem to have a red room or [red] furniture in my home—but colors are made more pleasurable by the things that are put next to them. The power of the vocabulary of color rests on the relational aspect because color is a vocabulary, just like language."

Spicy

Saffron, cinnamon, nutmeg, ginger: use these colors to add a dash of spice to your home decor. Earthen gold, heated red, warm brown, and a dash of bottle green combine to create an aromatic and exotic mix. Red can dominate a spicy color scheme, so decorate with deep shades, such as the rich reds of a Turkish carpet or the orange red of a Pompeiian wall. Take a cue from southern French interiors and use upholstery and table linens with the deep ochre yellow of Provençal fabrics.

The trick to working with such a heady and enticing mix is to add just enough spice to the blend. Decorate with neighboring colors from the warm side of the color wheel; begin with toasty, full-bodied reds and move toward piquant oranges paired with tangy mustard yellows. Mix warm, organic woods that are rough-hewn and chunky with hand-woven fabrics, such as kilim and dhurrie rugs, or paisley throws.

To prevent ruddy red and rich orange from overwhelming a spicy scheme, consider including chocolate brown and amber hues to create a mood that's both comfortable and lively. Combine raw earth hues with judicious amounts of the cool colors associated with the Eastern spice trade—cooling aquamarine, vivid lime, or glassy emerald green—to add contrast to a warm and spicy decorating scheme.

[ABOVE]
To temper a red-hot wall color, decorate with cooling shades of green, such as this blue-green and white checkerboard patterned tablecloth.

[RIGHT]
It is not only the ochre yellow wall color that heat up this living room; Rugs and throws from India and the Middle East, infused with exotic mixes of full-bodied red, yellow, blue, and green, add spice and comfort to a sunny corner. Use oriental, Navajo, or dhurrie rugs on floors to define conversation, group furniture, or add warmth to any room.

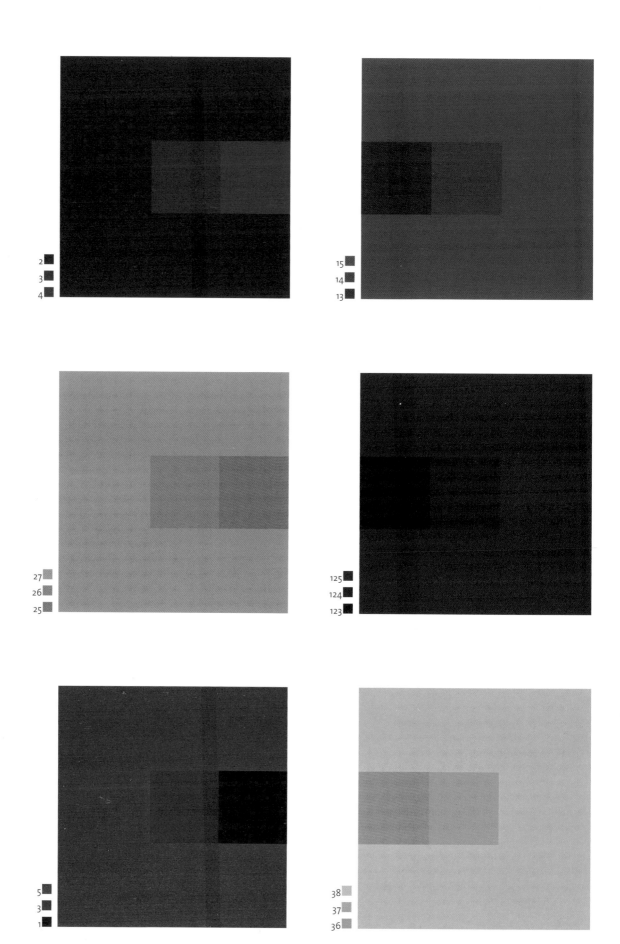

2
3
4

15
14
13

27
26
25

125
124
123

5
3
1

38
37
36

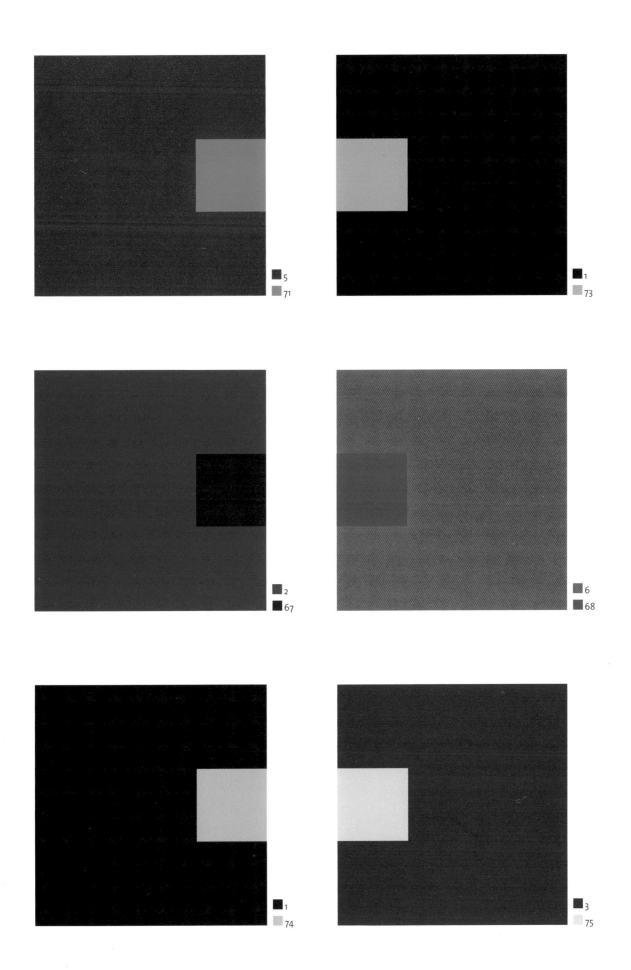

5
71

1
73

2
67

6
68

1
74

3
75

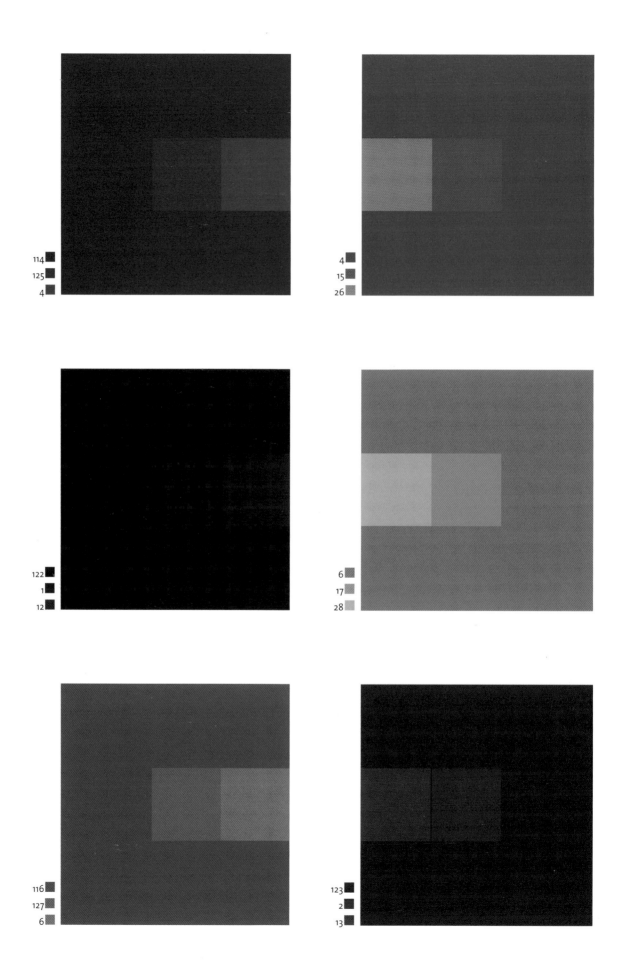

114
125
4

4
15
26

122
1
12

6
17
28

116
127
6

123
2
13

■ 5
■ 57

■ 4
■ 79

■ 1
■ 56

■ 2
■ 78

■ 13
■ 60

■ 15
■ 86

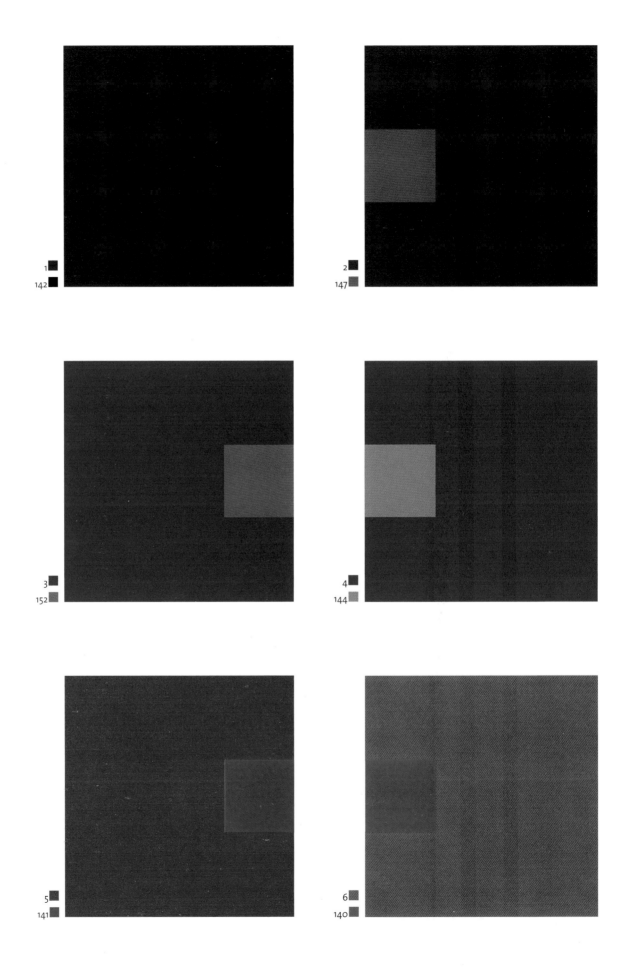

1
142

2
147

3
152

4
144

5
141

6
140

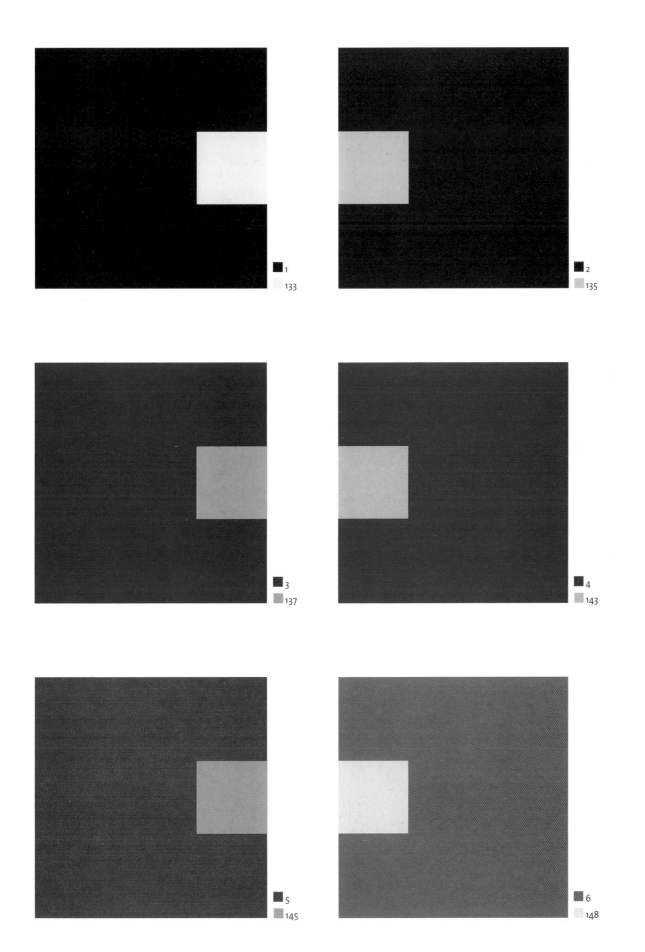

1
133

2
135

3
137

4
143

5
145

6
148

Decorating with
a spicy mix

A spicy decorating scheme is inclusive, warm, and eclectic. Its heady mix of earth colors complements and enhances a collection of international fabrics and accessories. Its warm tones heat up large, impersonal, or cold rooms. And its range of colors, from chili red to sari pink, with references to the Eastern spice trades of the eighteenth and nineteenth centuries, works well with an eclectic blend of contemporary furniture, family heirlooms, or prized antiques.

A kilim rug is the perfect floor covering for a spicy room; its earthy hues of red, yellow, and brown will work with several hot color schemes. Introduce small touches of a cooling green, such as green landscapes or accent pillows, to keep spicy colors from overheating.

Spicy **Tips**

• Vibrant and passionate, spicy hues look their best when used against a neutral backdrop, such as linen, jute, woven grass wall covering, canvas or linen upholstery. Conversely, to render a large, cold space warm and inviting, paint walls with spice tones to create a cozy sense of enclosure.

• Spicy hues enhance contemporary rooms as well as traditional ones. Stainless steel, glass surfaces, and shiny synthetic fabrics bring a modern glow and give spicy earth tones definition and gloss. Kilim pillows provide an authentic accent and add instant warmth to any room or nook. Although pillows in the kilim style are widely available at retailers, look for cushions or pillows covered with genuine patterns and dyes at purveyors of authentic kilim rugs.

• Spice tones blend well with organic shapes, well-worn books, and objects collected on travels. Coordinate these seasoned colors with your most cherished collections, small drawings or prints, natural materials, and fibers.

• To keep a spicy color combination from overheating, add small doses of cooling colors like turquoise and emerald green to the mix. Or lighten a wide expanse within the room with a neutral hue; for example, weathered limestone flooring provides a cooling base for a heated interior.

• Place small decorative accents on side tables, window sills, and ledges to complete the mood: Arrange cardamom pods, star anise, and the common cinnamon stick in shallow pottery bowls to introduce the welcoming aromas of exotic spice.

• Natural fibers and fabrics woven without dyes or artificial colorings provide a textured backdrop to enhance a spicy color scheme. Select from plain woven cotton; rough linen; jute and a growing array of woven grasses and palm fibers; or sturdy, unbleached canvas.

[ABOVE]
A spicy scheme can enliven the Colonial charm of an antique setting. As pretty as it is practical, the sturdy weave and glowing color of a kilim rug brings a bit of richness to the simplicity of the room.

[RIGHT]
A collection of antiques reminiscent of the Spice Trade—a celadon platter, Chinese sideboard, and brass candlesticks—add texture and history to the spicy background of a gold-stenciled, orange wall.

Exotic

Merge East and West for exotic decor that's perfect for dreaming grand dreams. Exotic and sensuous cinnabar—red with a hint of orange—is favored by the East. Feng shui experts consider this warm hue the color of recognition and fame. Distinctive and inviting, this ruddy red is a natural partner for brightly spiced oranges and muted earth tones. Shiny metallics, gold, and copper heighten and evoke the mystic properties of exotic cinnabar hues. Paired with whites and creams, this stimulating palette shimmers, while small amounts of soothing aquamarine cool this provocative blend. A lucky color, this enriched red is simultaneously minimal and grand, restrained and opulent—a hue of mystery and delight.

Exotic interiors span the globe and offer inspiration—from small Tibetan shrines to antiquities from China to intricate carvings from Japan. Recreate the look of a faraway place by blending select imports with contemporary low-level seating, floor cushions, and accessories with a nod to the Orient. Balance an exotic mix with a variety of woods, from dark rich hues to rosewood, bamboo, or teak. Continue the rich tradition of exchange between East and West by combining furnishing styles, art, and accessories. Counterbalance the grandeur of lacquer, gilt, brightly colored fabrics, and statuary with plain wood floors, tatami mats, and streamlined modern furnishings that hug the ground.

[RIGHT]
Use the basics of Feng Shui when decorating on exotic rooms. Combine light and dark furnishings, along with light and dark colors to bring energy and balance to a room.

16
14
12

13
17
16

14
16
12

12
16
18

18
14
12

17
16
13

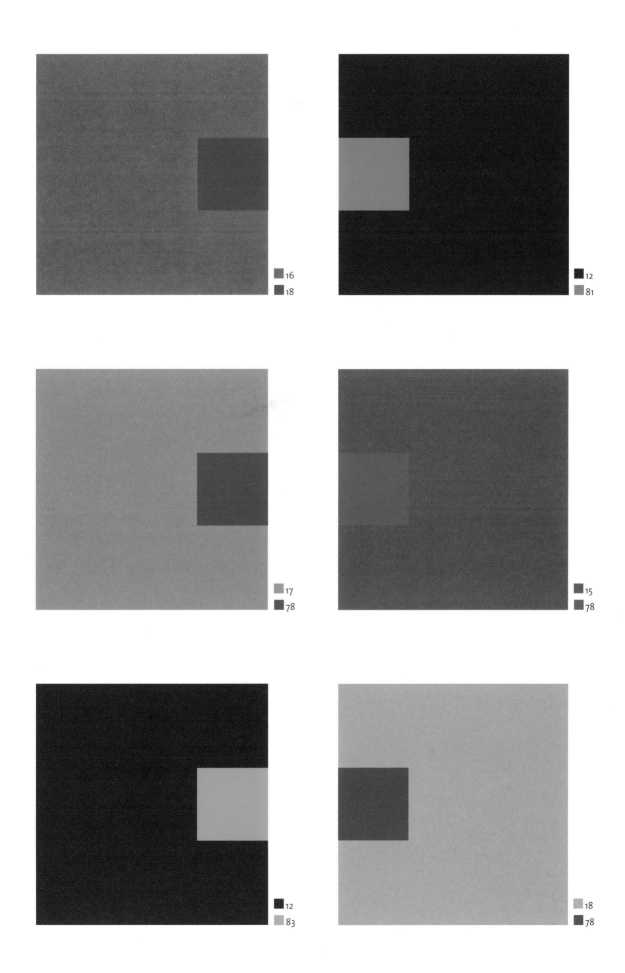

16
18

12
81

17
78

15
78

12
83

18
78

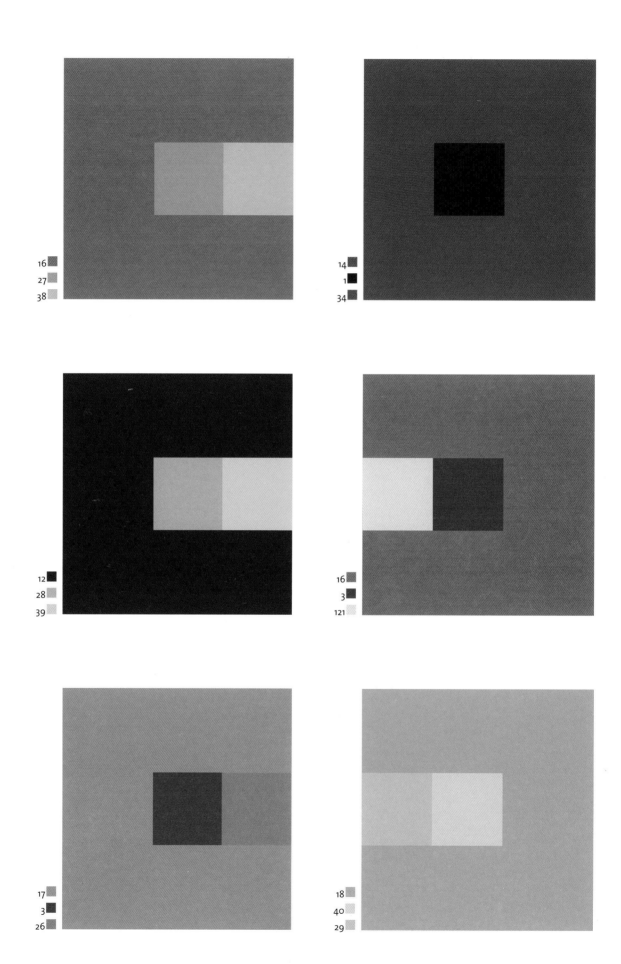

16
27
38

14
1
34

12
28
39

16
3
121

17
3
26

18
40
29

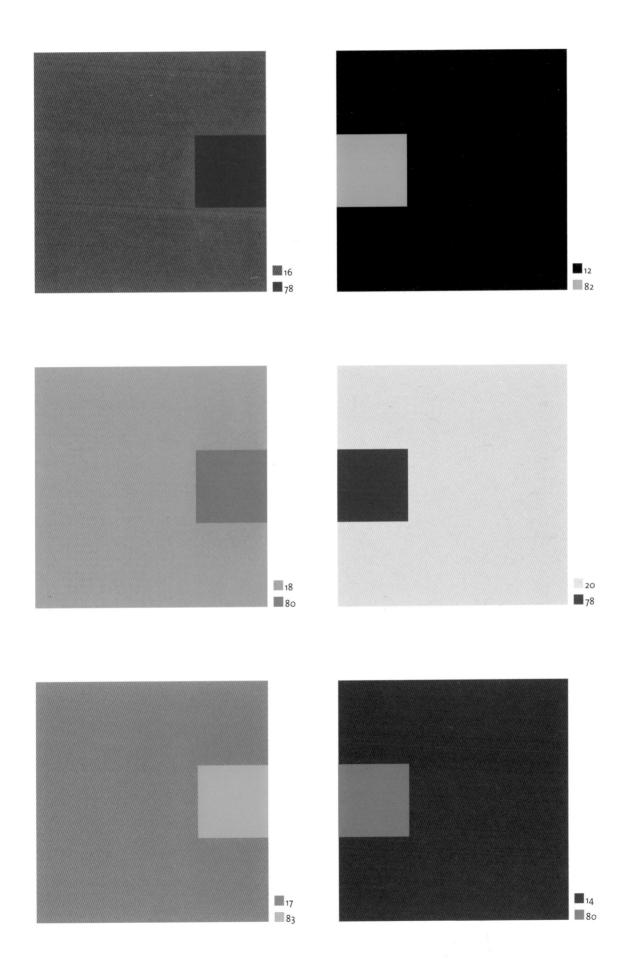

16
78

12
82

18
80

20
78

17
83

14
80

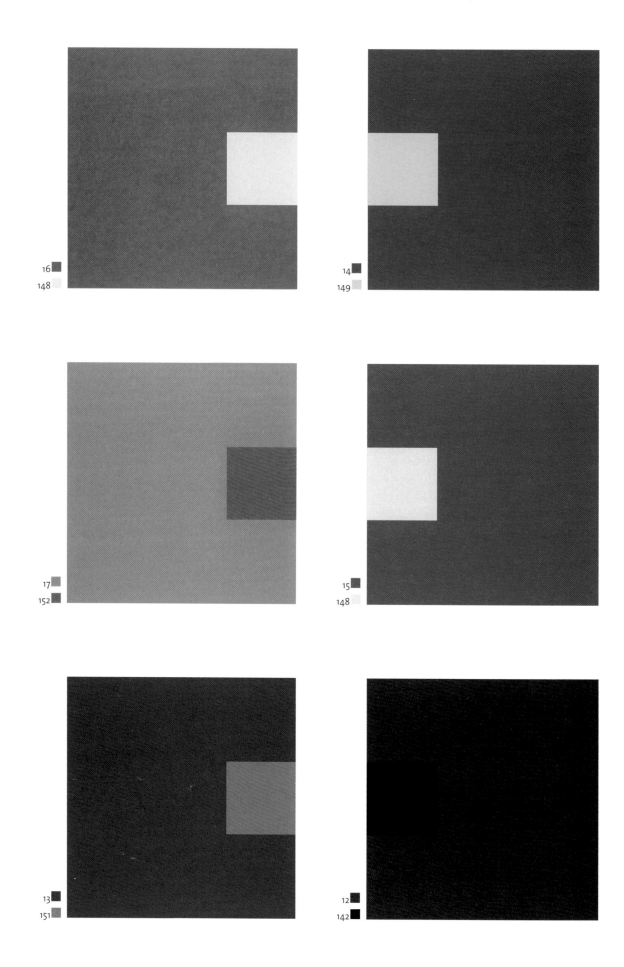

16
148

14
149

17
152

15
148

13
151

12
142

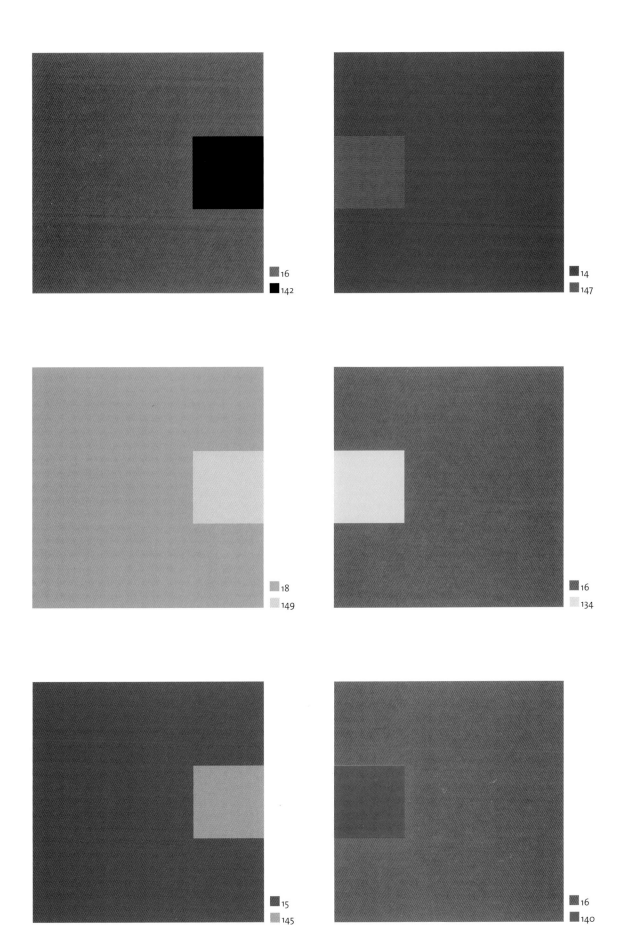

16
142

14
147

18
149

16
134

15
145

16
140

Decorating with an exotic mix

Foreign and familiar, an exotic decorating scheme is expressive and intriguing—creating a place for your spirit to soar, dreams to unfold, wishes to materialize. While an exotic decor requires thought and planning to cultivate, the provocative stimulation of this unusual decor is the well-earned reward. The soul of an exotic interior is the imaginative mood that overtakes you when you enter.

This exotic and eclectic mix of furnishings and accents is reminiscent of treasures collected along the old routes of the Spice Trade. Deep mahogany and burnt orange create a pleasant atmosphere, great for sparking the adventurous imagination.

Exotic **Tips**

•Use fragrance to enhance color within an exotic decor. Cinnamon and mandarin orange scents relate to fire-the element associated with a red-orange cinnabar hue. Choose from incense sticks, vaporizing oils, perfumed stones, and candles.

•Within an exotic interior, hanging fabric panels and curtains can act as room dividers, bringing large expanses of color to an environment. Also consider more neutral as well as traditional screens of translucent paper, bamboo, or carved wood.

•Particularly when planning an exotic interior with an Eastern influence, consider consulting a feng shui expert or book for guidance. The philosophy of feng shui is to live in harmony with your environment so that the energy surrounding you works for you rather than against you. Attention to the placement of objects and furnishings when decorating is one of feng shui's basic principles. It is suggested that you combine equal amounts of light and dark furnishings, along with light and dark colors, to bring positive energy and balance to a room.

•Moderate-to low-priced imports, such as paper lanterns; fabrics that feature small mirrors and embroidery; carved figures; and candle holders, are widely available. Go global by carefully selecting several pieces to blend with more expensive and substantial finds, such as a painstakingly crafted piece of Japanese cabinetry. Classic choices from the East include staircase chests (tansu), display cabinets, calligraphy boxes, and wheeled chests.

•Combine sleek decorative lacquerware and opulent accessories with simple furnishings for a yin/yang balance. Seek out blue-green (the complement of red-orange) when selecting visual accents to bring to a room.

•Recycle a couch by covering with a shimmering satin sheet. Don't sew or cut the fabric unless you absolutely must-just bunch and tuck. The loose fit is part of the look and makes your impromptu slipcover easy to launder.

[ABOVE]
Merge East and West furnishing styles. Muted, dark stained wicker with a matte lacquer finish is a natural partner for this Asian-inspired Ottoman-style table that rises only inches above the floor.

[RIGHT]
Infused with the exoticism and mystery of the East, this mix of subdued colors and the unadorned wood of the floor and furnishings brings harmonious atmosphere to a quiet retreat.

essentially orange

Combine orange and pure white to creat
a space that is peaceful and bright.

Orange is easy to integrate into a color scheme because it is compatible with so many colors. Just a touch of orange in a room can dramatically alter the spirit and energy level. As you move through this chapter, think about how you might adapt one or more orange hues into your home palette. It can, by its dramatic tonal range, be a very useful decorating tool.

The Orange Range

Think of a summer sunset and you will be reminded of orange's beautiful range—from the deepest red-orange down to the softest, palest yellow-orange. At its darkest tone, orange is energized and emits warmth; at its lightest, when it moves from salmon to peach, it's as peaceful as dawn. Orange works in any room of the home and can be used with both dark and light furnishings, contemporary or traditional.

Bringing Orange Into the Scene

There are many ways you can introduce orange into your décor, be it just an accent to another color, or as the dominant color in your design palette. Here are a few ideas:

• Introduce orange at eye level under kitchen cabinets to brighten the work area.

• Paint the inside of a windowless walk-in pantry a shade of burnt orange and accent with yellow.

• Use a cheery shade of yellow-orange as the backdrop for your sun porch or sunroom, and add accents of green and gold. Mix in a floral print via pillows or seating Consider orange taking the lead in a young girl's or boy's bedroom or bathroom. Accent with deep shades of blue and green or pink and yellow.

• Take the richest hue of orange and brighten up the stairway to your basement—save yellow or bright blue for the banister!

• Pull swatches of the palest shade of orange and pair it with an equally pale blue-green for a spa-like bathroom, dressing room, or peaceful, feminine study.

• Find a fabric you love that integrates shades of orange and use it as a bed canopy, window treatment, or to recover your favorite reading chair and footstool. Consider painting one wall of that room in a solid shade of dark orange and the other three in a very pale shade.

Orange Combinations

Remember, orange is versatile and highly compatible. Try using three or more of these colors in fabrics, floor treatments, artwork, or other decorative elements.
• Orange and yellow
• Orange and green
• Orange and blue
• Orange and purple
• Orange and black
• Orange and pink
• Orange and red

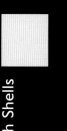

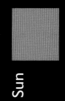

Beach Shells   Sunrise   Sunset   Basic Orange   Summer Sun   Sand Dune   Terra Cotta

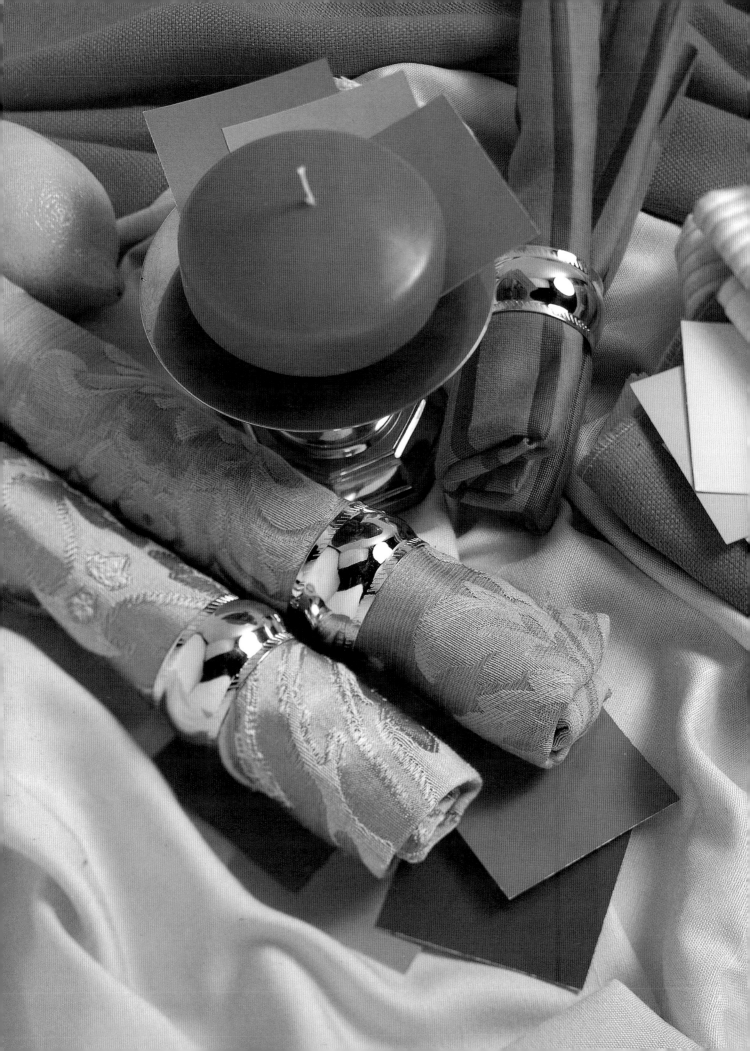

Gold and burnt-orange give these spaces a pleasant color base for furnishings and art. Introducing earthy tones like brown, gold, and moss green in couch pillows and accessories maintains a peaceful mood.

When you want a color to take the palette lead you don't have to cover all the walls with it. Just one wall will do, as you see in this bedroom with an Asian flair.

CELESTE COOPER, A NEW YORK– AND BOSTON-BASED INTERIOR DESIGNER:

"I think color is a very personal thing. For instance, I hate orange but it certainly works for Hermes! I have never refused to work with a client's favorite color but I might, for instance, try to use that orange as an accent and not on the walls!"

KELLY HOPPEN, A LONDON-BASED INTERIOR DESIGNER:

"Orange, if it is burnt, is an amazing color, and works well with neutrals."

MARY DOUGLAS DRYSDALE, A WASHINGTON, D.C.–BASED INTERIOR DESIGNER:

"I love warm colors. The palette I feel comfortable with is pumpkin to yellow. I love them because they're vigorous and optimistic. There's the relationship to the sun and warmth. On a sunny day we think we'll conquer the world and if we come into a space and the color energizes, it reinforces optimism."

**NEW YORK–BASED ARCHITECT
R. SCOTT BROMLEY:**

"I love orange—it's the color of love!"

**ARCHITECT HEATHER FAULDING:
NEW YORK**

"Color is and should be the story of everything."

**ALEXANDRA STODDARD,
A NEW YORK–BASED INTERIOR DESIGNER:**

"One of the things I feel strongly about is a lot of people who are afraid of color find these glamorous names for ugly colors. For example they call them cinnamon, and the color really could be called sick puppy poop! Put that all over a wall and I think it will smell bad!"

**NORTH CAROLINA–BASED ARCHITECT
SARAH SUSANKA:**

"The neat thing about paint is you can change it. I encourage people to get a piece of sheetrock or plywood if they're painting outside, and use the color they're contemplating on a large enough piece (near other things) to better evaluate it."

Orange is as appropriate for a formal living room as it is for a child's playroom. In this space, billowy tangerine curtains move like wet brushstrokes of color down the lemony walls, creating an enticing retreat.

Here again, orange take the lead, this time in a living room. The dark color against the all-white furnishings creates a crisp, neat space that's also peaceful.

Dynamic

Orange is sporty, active, and dynamic—a favorite of mid-century modernists. When using this energetic color, be wary of overpowering even the most wide open living space. However, selective splashes of dramatic orange will brighten, and enliven small and large interiors. Team orange with red-orange and yellow-orange for an analogous combination or with shocking pinks for a feminine mix that sizzles. Saturated lime green is another welcome addition to a powerful palette that focuses on orange. If your choices feel overheated, judicious amounts of complementary blues or lots of natural cream and white will cool this palette.

Sculptural furnishings of plastic, metal, molded wood, tubular metal, and glass work well within a kinetic design that features a stimulating palette. Retro fabrics and furniture styles add to the dynamic. Look for new interpretations of vintage furnishings that use biomorphic curves, such as a boomerang or kidney-shaped coffee table. Fabrics that feature 1950s space-age icons such as amoebas and atomic kitsch bring energy and humor to a lively interior. Modernize with a lively tangerine sectional and pillows in new earth tones.

Multipurpose, multi-task living is a dynamic component of modern life. Expansive rooms—where the majority of home living takes place—continue to grow in popularity.
Open-air life requires special attention to furniture placement, storage solutions, and room divisions. Select basic, clean-lined storage components that can be reconfigured as your needs change. Group furnishings away from the walls to create cozy centers, and use movable screens or sliding doors to create divisions within a spacious interior or to enlarge a small room.

[ABOVE]
A coat of tangerine orange paint paired with inexpensive natural wood shelving is one way to create a flexible storage area that's also dynamic. Another is to paint the interior of a cabinet that has transparent glass doors a sassy hue to add interest and surprise.

[RIGHT]
A dynamic scheme can be founded on a few bright accents without requiring an all-over wash of color. Here, freewheeling slices of bright, saturated hues give bold energy to an open space.

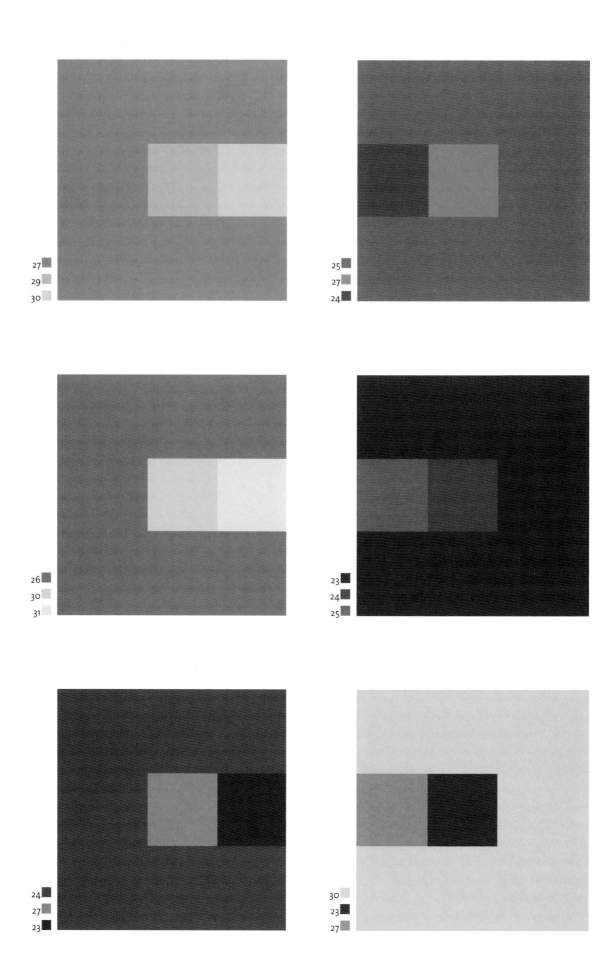

27
29
30

25
27
24

26
30
31

23
24
25

24
27
23

30
23
27

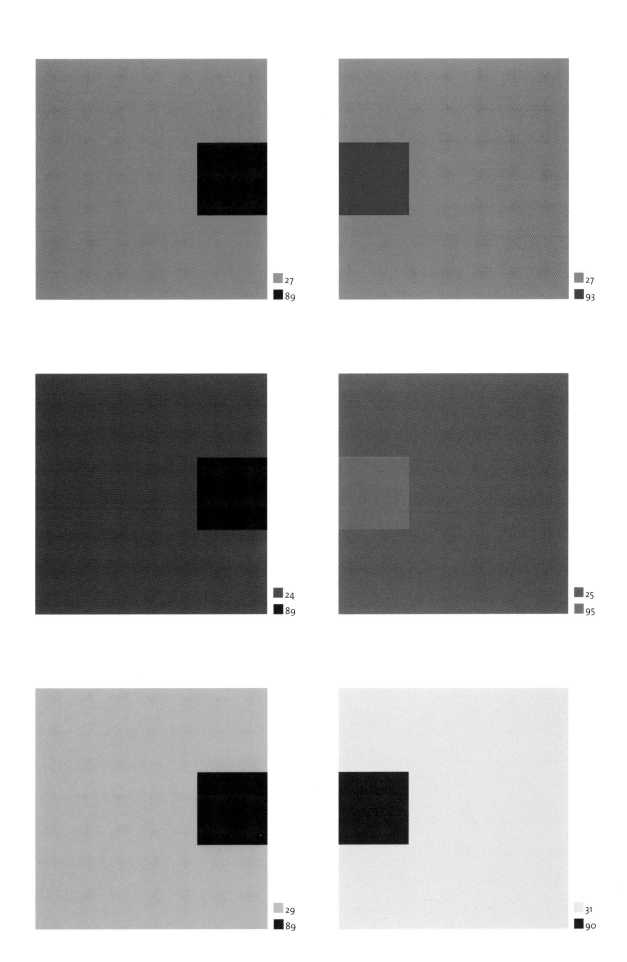

27
89

27
93

24
89

25
95

29
89

31
90

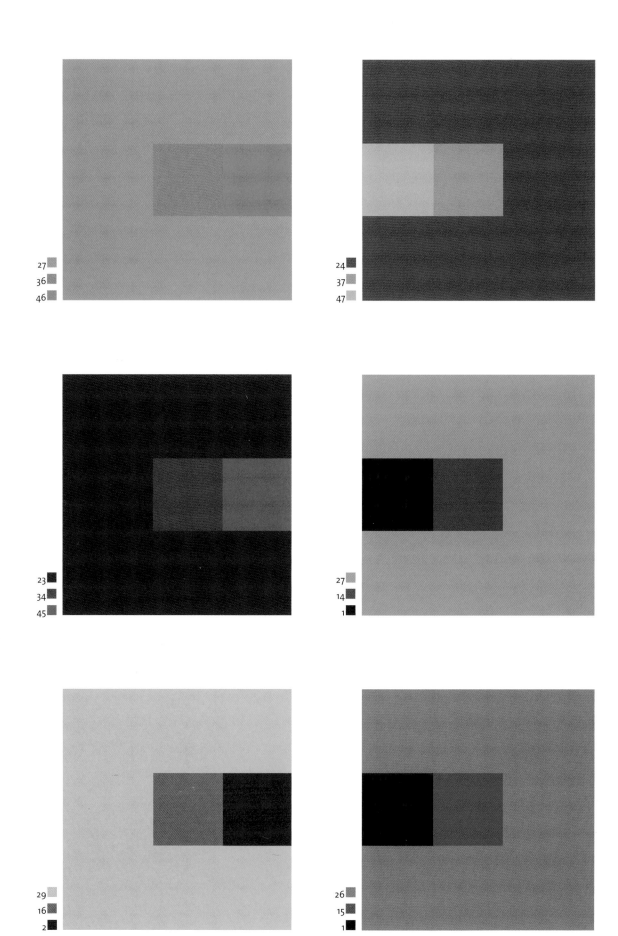

ANALOGOUS

27
36
46

24
37
47

23
34
45

27
14
1

29
16
2

26
15
1

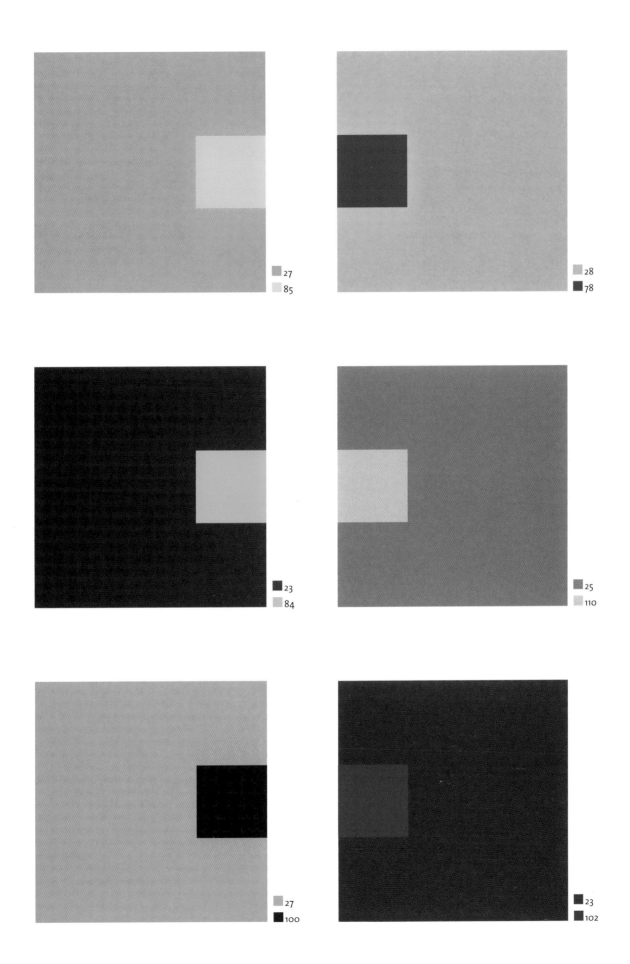

27
85

28
78

23
84

25
110

27
100

23
102

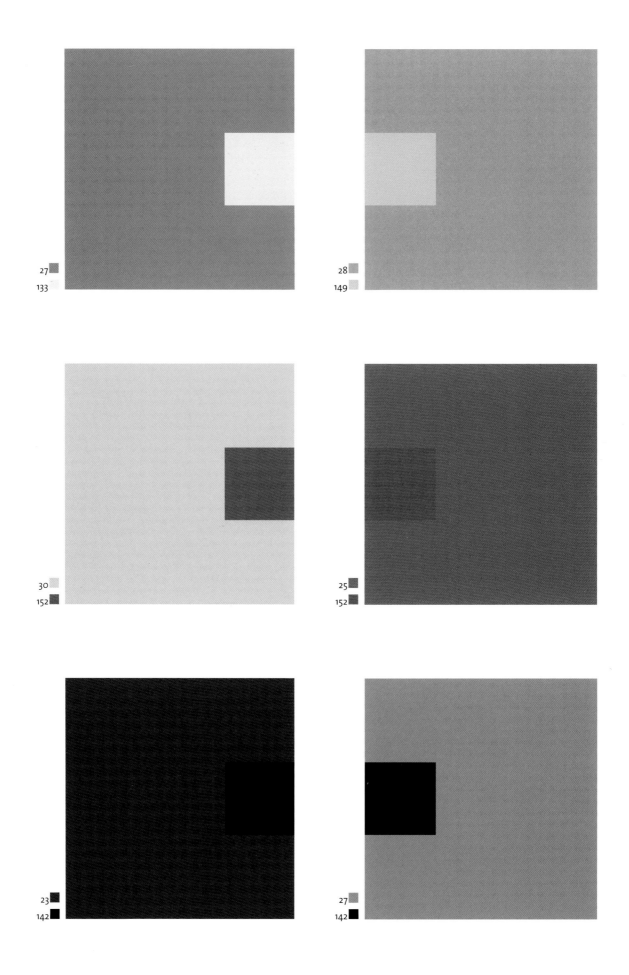

27
133

28
149

30
152

25
152

23
142

27
142

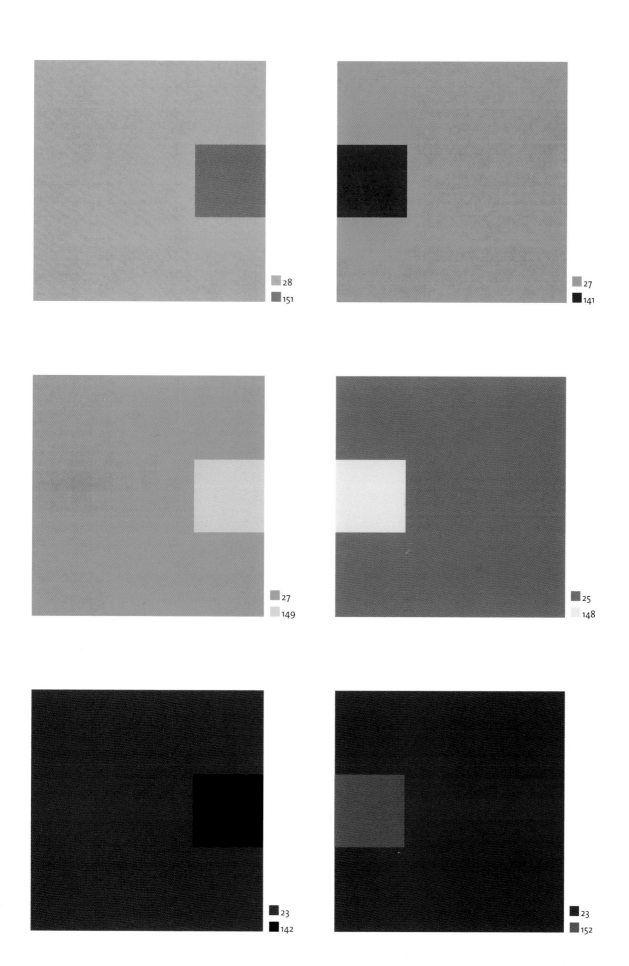

28
151

27
141

27
149

25
148

23
142

23
152

Decorating with a dynamic mix

A dynamic color palette is sassy and bright. Its

exuberant blend of spirited colors brings

both large and small areas to life.

Retro accessories, vintage fabrics, and freshly

interpreted furnishings set the stage for the

drama of life. Be bold: dare to mix poppy orange,

cinnabar reds, and lively 1970s hues with a

neutral background or complementary hues for

explosive design.

Efficient storage solutions offer a dynamic option for creating
a bedroom that also functions as a personal center for well-
being. White bedding, natural woods, and rattan wall-to-wall
flooring recede to allow the simplicity of two orange pillows
to dominate this multi-tasking room.

Dynamic **Tips**

•Pulling furnishings away from the wall will make a large or small room appear larger. Use a bright orange area rug to create a dynamic conversational grouping. Whether your room is large or small, try floating your couch or sofa away from the wall.

•Get more function out of your couch by placing a console or sofa table behind it to store and stack books or hold a reading lamp.

•Use focused light to create drama and spotlight dashes of vivid color in your interior. Consider pole lamps, hanging ball lamps covered with translucent rice paper, or halogen lighting. Use spots and dimmers to strategically light colorful furnishings, accents, walls, and artwork. Place inexpensive can lights on the floor behind furnishings or indoor plantings for dynamic uplighting.

•Transform a large or small space into a high-performance environment tailored to your life. First determine your day-to-day, short-and long-term needs, then use modular shelving and organizers to keep everyday items readily available. Short-term items can be stored in rattan baskets or galvanized metal bins, while industrial utility shelves on wheels, rolling carts, and bins provide flexible long-term storage and can easily be pushed out of sight.

•Hunt for colorful accessories that recall the mid-twentieth century, such as biomorphic vases, iconic supergraphics (think big dots, psychedelics, and arrows), atomic wall clocks, and "Jetson" style appliances. Well-placed dashes of vibrant color add energy and vigor to a dynamic decor.

[ABOVE]
Transform a small space, such as this bath, with a dynamic mix of blue and green tiles beneath orange walls.

[RIGHT]
Use complementary colors such as these vivid blue pillows and lamp shades to add interest and energy to a dynamic decor.

Natural

Decorating with natural materials creates a haven for modern living that is soothing to the soul. Today we desire serenity and peace within ourselves and our environments.
Restful environments often use gentle palettes that seek their inspiration from the land. Colors that draw their inspiration from the earth, such as warm ruddy browns, golden mineral hues, or pale eggshell and bone tints, create an atmosphere of calm.

Use the earth tones of materials such as unbleached linen and fabrics colored with natural dyes when composing your own living environment. Discover the infinite variety of yellow-orange paints and the moods they create. Light tints of yellow-orange will enlarge and brighten a small room or entry, creating a welcoming sense of space. Deeper honeyed shades bring warmth to a great room with high ceilings and humanize large open spaces. Select a dense caramel paint to create a cozy meditative environment. For a natural look, seek furnishings that are designed in the unadorned Shaker style, garden-influenced pieces costructed from wicker, cane, and bamboo, or simple hand-carved furniture.

A naturally based interior is the undisputed workhorse of interior decorating. Creamy walls paired with wooden floors are to an interior decorator what canvas is to an artist. The simplicity of plain pine floors and buff walls is the perfect base to build upon. Impact colors such as Chianti red and amber orange can be introduced in the form of changeable soft furnishings like pillow coverings and slipcovers. Seasonal accessories can also add interest to a natural decor—for summer, imagine oversized candles placed in trays surrounded by a mound of recently found seashells, or for autumn a sheath of cane or wheat bound at the base with raffia to fill an urn or vase.

[ABOVE]
Floor coverings for all-natural fibers such as jute and coir can be found in a wide variety of shapes and colors. If asked, many home outlets will cut and bind these inexpensive rugs to your specifications.

[RIGHT]
Balance and Simplicity. Use a bundle or two of natural cane reeds as a seasonal touch in the late summer and early autumn months.

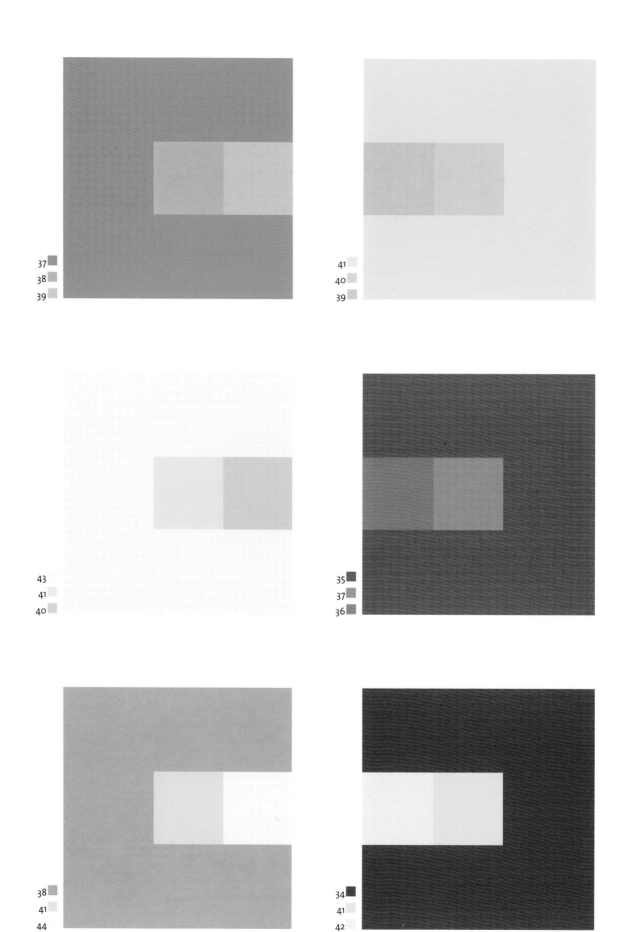

37
38
39

41
40
39

43
41
40

35
37
36

38
41
44

34
41
42

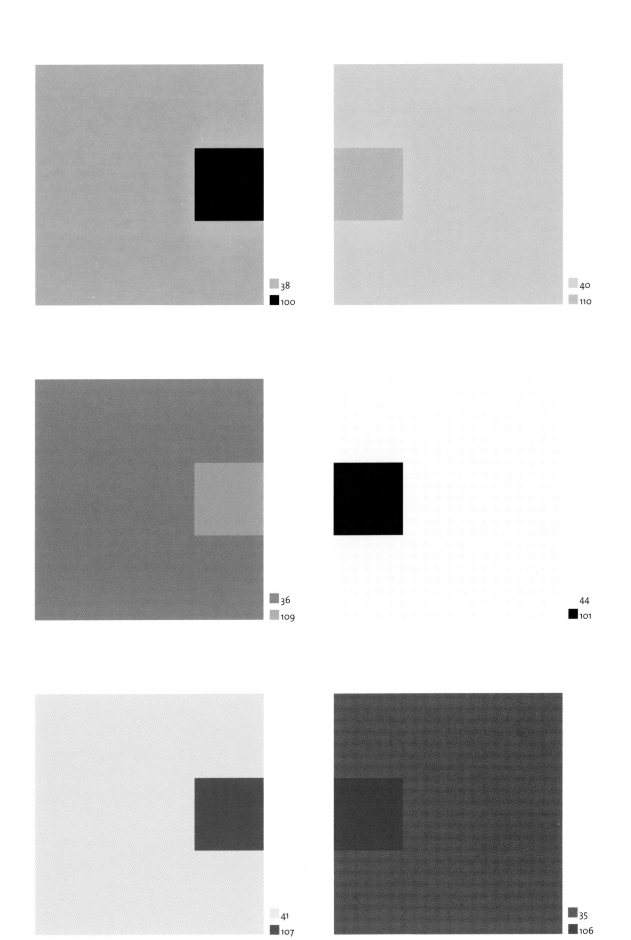

38
100

40
110

36
109

44
101

41
107

35
106

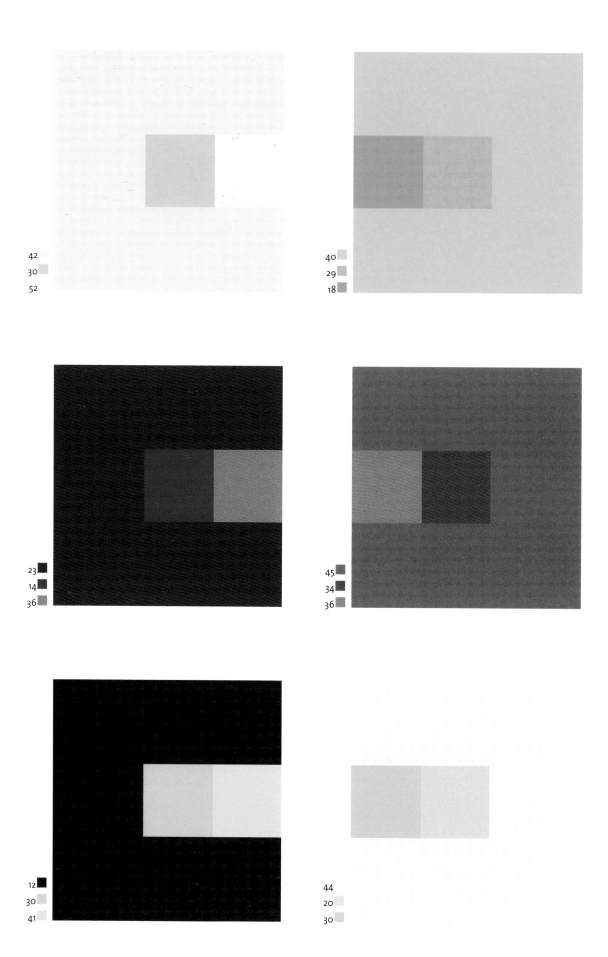

42
30
52

40
29
18

23
14
36

45
34
36

12
30
41

44
20
30

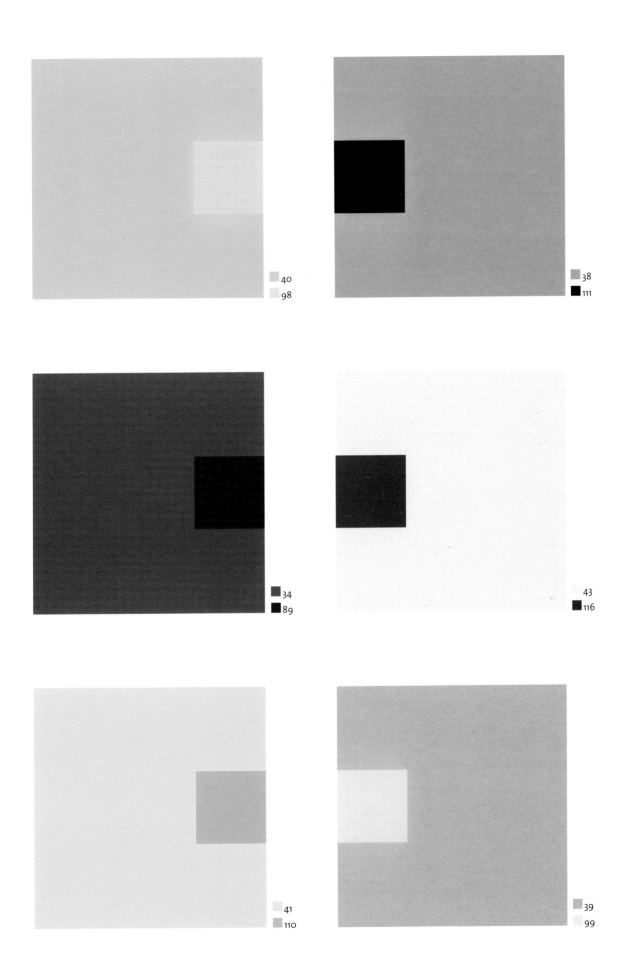

40
98

38
111

34
89

43
116

41
110

39
99

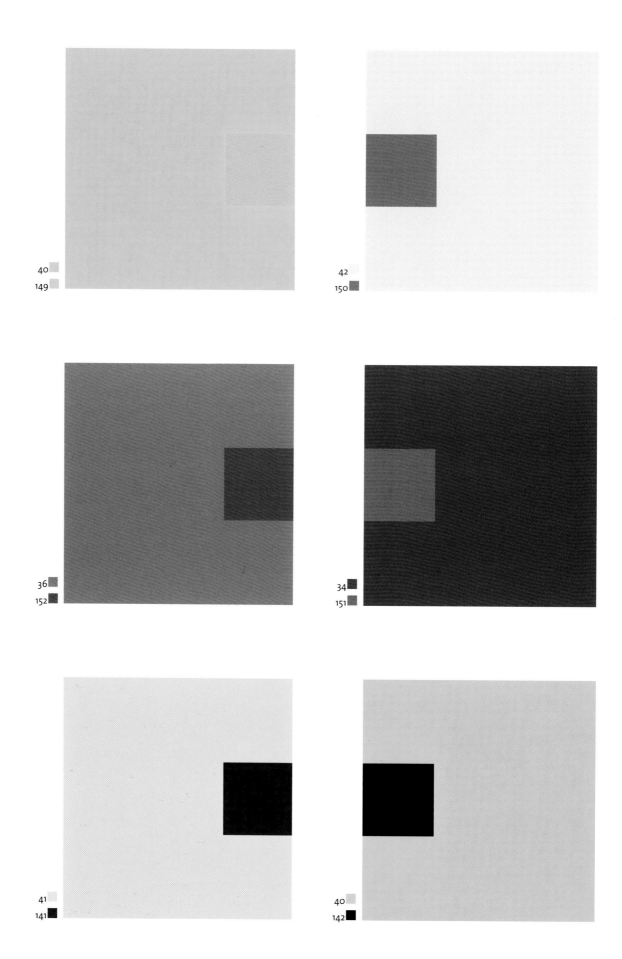

40
149

42
150

36
152

34
151

41
141

40
142

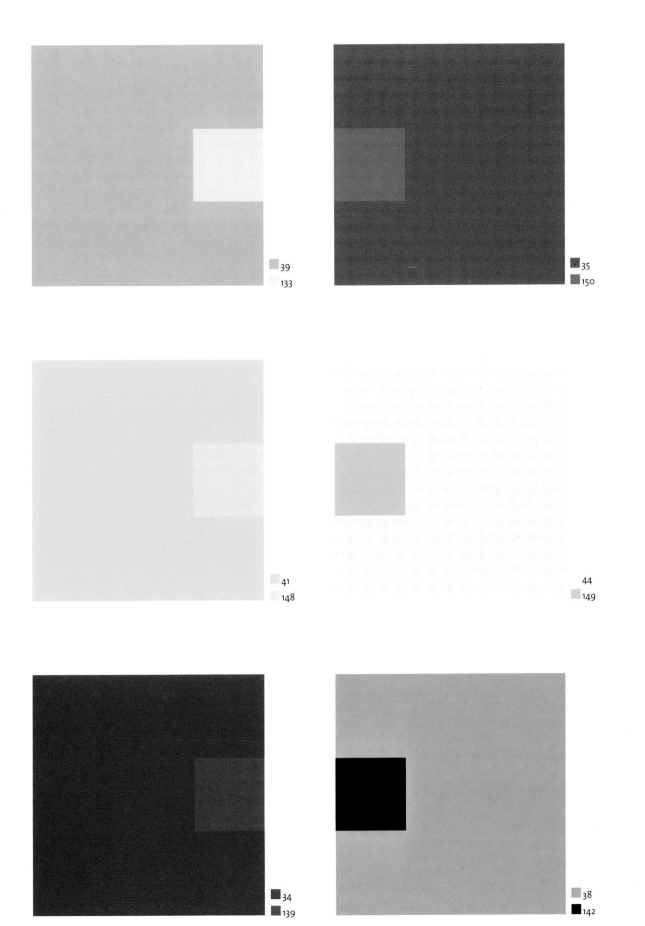

39
133

35
150

41
148

44
149

34
139

38
142

Decorating with a natural mix

Welcoming and calming, a golden-hued palette also emphasizes texture. Delicately handwoven fabrics, natural fiber floor coverings, and crisp buttery cottons will all add interest to a simply inspired decor. The smooth quality of burnished coppers, ambers, and golds work to ground an earth-based scheme. Watery blues and sky-inspired violets combined with natural sunlight bring life and energy to a natural color scheme. Balance these basic colors of the earth with texture, shape, and seasonal accessories for an atmosphere that reflects your personal taste.

Faux beams of rustic wood are used to give this enclosed dining room an outdoor, natural mood. The monochromatic table and chairs provide a stage for dramatic dining.

Natural **Tips**

•Warm a room with the rich colors of glowing embers by grouping furniture around a fireplace. This creates an instant oasis of calm, particularly in a busy open room. Generous low seating, oversized coffee tables, a variety of cozy throws, and softly glowing embers from the fire will enhance the feeling of well-being that a natural interior bestows.

•Use paint to create an accent wall. Paint one wall a rich butter cream hue. Consider painting adjoining rooms with analogous colors, such as saffron yellow or nutmeg orange. Contemplate painting moldings, window and door trim a darker contrasting shade instead of the standard white. A saturated, glossy olive green or shiny chocolate brown will create depth and interest when paired with soft honey or cream hued walls.

•Select your furnishings for a natural room carefully—every item need not be a "star." First determine what pieces will be background and which pieces will be featured. For example, an unattractive dining table can be covered with a plain unbleached cotton cloth and a natural linen table runner, allowing the focal point to become a set of woven wicker chairs.

•Everyday tea can be used to dye fabrics naturally. Experiment with rose hip, hibiscus, and chamomile to achieve a variety of shades. Ruddy natural hues can be achieved with rose hips tea while more yellow to gold tones result from hibiscus and chamomile. Dampen the fabric completely (cotton blends work best) and submerge in a tea bath until the desired tint is achieved.

•Inexpensive canvas Roman shades or bamboo blinds may be all you need for window treatments in a room that features a natural palette. Alternatively, consider leaving windows bare, as natural interiors embrace light.

•Create form and function within a natural room by using wicker baskets of assorted sizes to store toys, magazines, and the clutter of everyday life. Baskets can be hung, stacked, or nested when not in use.

[ABOVE]
Clean and honest, the inter—related decorating styles of Shaker, mission, and arts and crafts lend themselves to the unpretentious colors of the earth. On this bed, standard sized pillows in plain cotton covers are arranged vertically to bring height to the overall look of this simple bedding.

[RIGHT]
A rich layering of textures and colors taken straight from forest and earth—glowing natural hues of sunset orange warm the rough stone of a wash basin and its base of smooth wooden planks.

primarily yellow

Yellow makes a perfect "neutral": warm[e] and more sumptuous than white, it work[s] well as a backdrop for dark or black furnishings, and heightens the honey tones in polished wood floors

How can anyone not like yellow? It says so much to us that is positive. We smile when the sun comes out, and when it sinks down into the horizon. And, nearly everyone on the planet photographs yellow's many moods in nature. It is a color of cheer, warmth, and light, for sure, and it's no wonder fabric, wallpaper, and paint manufacturers give us so much to choose from in the yellow range. Used sparingly or not, yellow glows on—rarely creating a negative mood in our space.

The Yellow Range

Yellow's range moves from green-yellow to bright lemon-yellow, to golden—all the way down to the faintest shades of butter.

As a green-yellow, it is commonly used as an accent color or to saturate an ultra—modern, sculptural furnishing that's making a big design statement. Think of green—yellow as more of a focused hue that's got its color antenna up for what it complements. Some trendy, hot designers have been using this shade in the new, hip hotels and restaurants, and it is making its way into the more confident color lovers' homes.

Brighter, purer yellows that remind us of buttercups or daisies are often a good fit in period rooms, where they set up an engaging visual plane of contrast with deep, dark woods. Rooms seem to glow in these tones and with snowdrift white trims, and ceilings, bright yellow presents a crisp, clean, energized space. These same hues also find their way into kitchens, where the warmth of the hearth, and the rays of morning sun combine to sustain a cheery palette.

With the paler yellow hues, the mood moves from cheer to a calm, steady glow. The more white added, the more distant the yellow, and the more latitude to accent and contrast.

Bringing Yellow Into the Scene

There are no rules on where yellow works best in a home. In fact, it's one color that really looks as attractive in a bedroom as it does a den. Just remember, the intensity of the color sets the mood.

Imagine how a den that lights up with the late afternoon setting sun will look in a deep, golden yellow. That color will take the natural light and emphasize warmth year round. In summer, you can tone it down by introducing other cooler accent colors via throw pillows or curtains in a new palette.

Take advantage of yellow's intensity by using it in a low—light hallway, entryway, kitchen, or tiny powder room. Accent it with other warm colors like red, orange, or peach to direct the yellow focus. Turn to shades of green and brown as accents and you can create a more earthy, calm, casual mood in a library, study, or sunroom. Whatever you choose, you can blend in snow white, other shades of yellow, and even black to punctuate architectural details.

Yellow Combinations

Try finding real examples of these to help you visualize how well they work together and spark your imagination:
• Yellow and red
• Yellow and green
• Yellow and purple
• Yellow and orange
• Yellow and blue
• Yellow and pink
• Yellow and lilac

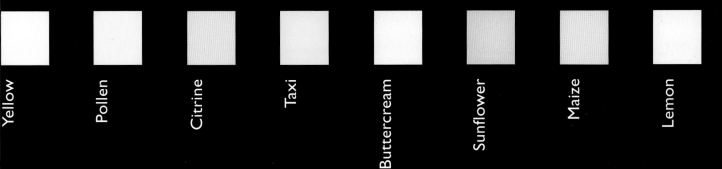

Yellow   Pollen   Citrine   Taxi   Buttercream   Sunflower   Maize   Lemon

What are you looking to create in your room? How do you want to feel? In this bedroom, a nature-themed palette of green and yellow with dark woods is peaceful and warm.

If you use yellow as the main color in your window treatment, you can make a dramatic statement—especially if you have a room with high ceilings like this one. Also, if you are in a north-facing room, the color can help you get through low-light days. Keeping the ceiling white gives the room more light, and using an open floral with complementary colors really ties up a look.

If you choose not to paint a wall yellow, but you would like the effect it brings, look for art to do the job. These panels of yellow not only satisfy the inhabitant's craving for yellow, they set off the soft blues that make up a secondary color theme.

JEAN TOWNSEND, PROFESSIONAL PAINTER

"I'm naturally drawn to a high-key color palette in my artwork. But the for the colors I prefer to live with, those would be too bright. I'm most comfortable around old things, weathered, with dings, that have some sign of hav-ing had a life, and when that happens to satur-ated colors, it mellows them a bit. That's when you get old-feeling colors like Sicilian yellow! In order to get colors without bite you have to gray them down, and to do that you add their complement to the paint. So to get yellow to be softer, you put a little purple in the paint."

KELLY HOPPEN,
LONDON INTERIOR DESIGNER:

"Yellow is a color I never use if I can help it. I always think it looks tacky, and is very difficult to use as well."

ANTHONY ANTINE, NEW YORK–BASED
INTERIOR DESIGNER:

"Yellow is my favorite color. It makes a room always have sunshine, and makes me happy. I like it buttery and creamy, I find other versions too harsh."

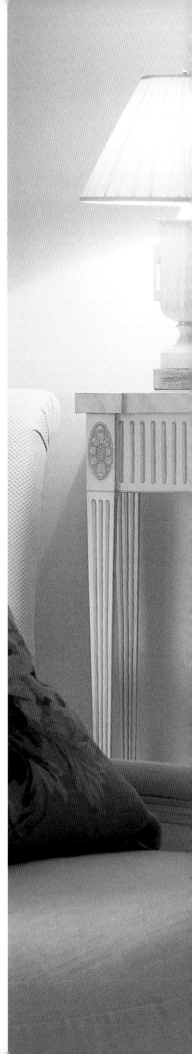

KAKI HOCKERSMITH, INTERIOR DESIGNER FOR THE WHITE HOUSE UNDER THE CLINTON ADMINISTRATION:

"The common denominator at the White House is yellow or gold, and that's a happy, sunny color. They [President Clinton and his wife Hillary] really like color, and natural light which is the reason they enjoy bright pastels..."

EVA DEWITZ, A BOSTON-BASED INTERIOR DESIGNER:

"I find that lemon yellow is very harsh and in a north-facing room, will actually seem strangely cold. For pale yellow I like the yellow-cream color of rich vanilla ice cream or I use yellow with a hint of orange to retain warmth of the color no matter the compass direction of the room."

TREENA CROCHET, A BOSTON-BASED INTERIOR DESIGNER:

"I'm from the South and I painted my entire Boston home in shades of yellow. I need the sunshine, and when I don't get it I get real sluggish. I used four variations of yellow in my home, and now when it's gray outside, I'm energetic!"

Whenever you take color to its palest form, you give yourself the most freedom to go elegant. Buttery yellow walls provide the perfect frame for soft, curvaceous, furnishings.

To create a clean, crisp, modern look, consider lemon-yellow walls. This will frame and accentuate furnishings and art.

ZINA GLAZEBROOK, A NEW YORK–BASED
INTERIOR DESIGNER

"It's wonderful when you have a blank canvas,
like a guest room—take a big color leap here.
It's not a room you're in all the time... For
rooms you are in a lot, it's nice to have them
clean, and neutral, especially those filled with
everyday objects. It keeps it peaceful."

ANTHONY ANTINE, A NEW YORK–BASED
INTERIOR DESIGNER:

"If I had a dark hallway with one window
I would paint the hallway yellow with a linen
white trim and a bright white ceiling. I'd keep
the stairs natural or walnut. The darker the
floor with light walls, the more height."

WASHINGTON, D.C.–BASED INTERIOR
DESIGNER MARY DOUGLAS DRYSDALE:

"Everyone underestimates the power of yellow.
It's strong. You take the light value of it and all
of a sudden this mousy color turns into a lion,
so you have to be very careful with the hue
you choose."

**What better way to brighten and add
cheer to a room than with lemony yellow?
Keeping the palette simple by adding only
white to the scheme can also be calming.**

Luminescent

A luminescent interior shines with hospitality and warmth. When you decorate with the luster of yellow, you illuminate your home. The brightest hue of the color wheel, yellow beams, growing more radiant with the addition of white. An assortment of creams, from ecru and oyster to rich shades of caramel and honey, enhance yellow's appreciation of natural light. Blend warm, glowing yellows with yellow-orange and orange for a glowing, analogous color scheme. Pair with light dove gray for the semblance of candlelight on a cold winter day. Strong, robust yellows combine well with jewel toned greens and indigo blues. When mixed with yellow, warm browns inspire a retro 1970s' mood.

Look to the French, masters of style and light, for inspiration when decorating an interior centered around yellow. Traditional furnishings like simple country French, or even a slightly more formal mood, suit the disposition of a yellow-focused room. To accent a luminous decor, select gilt mirrors and picture frames; accent tables of rich wood or shimmering metal and sculpted wire; translucent window treatments and tapestries. Create an ever-changing mood with reflective glass, mirrors, and metals, which all combine well with yellow to achieve an uplifting luminescent scheme. Wallpaper that mimics fabrics, such as jacquard or damask, and seasonal velvety slipcovers bring luxury to a luminous decor. Decorate with yellow to further illuminate rooms with large windows that capture the early morning sun. As the day progresses, light candles and flickering votives to add the friendly glow of candlelight. Choose lamps for low-level lighting and replace tired light fixtures with vintage reproductions that feature frosted shades and milk glass to maintain a welcoming glow into the night.

[RIGHT]
Position furnishings so that they are bathed in the light of day like this country French table that features tone on tone linens in tints of radiant yellow. Use blinds, drapes, or slipcovers and tablecloths to protect from damaging rays.

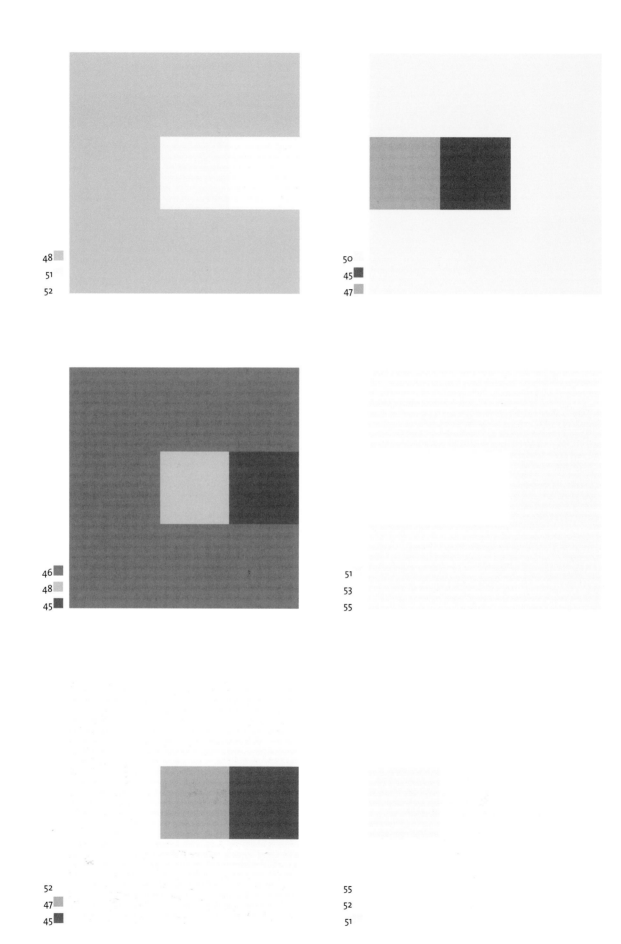

48
51
52

50
45
47

46
48
45

51
53
55

52
47
45

55
52
51

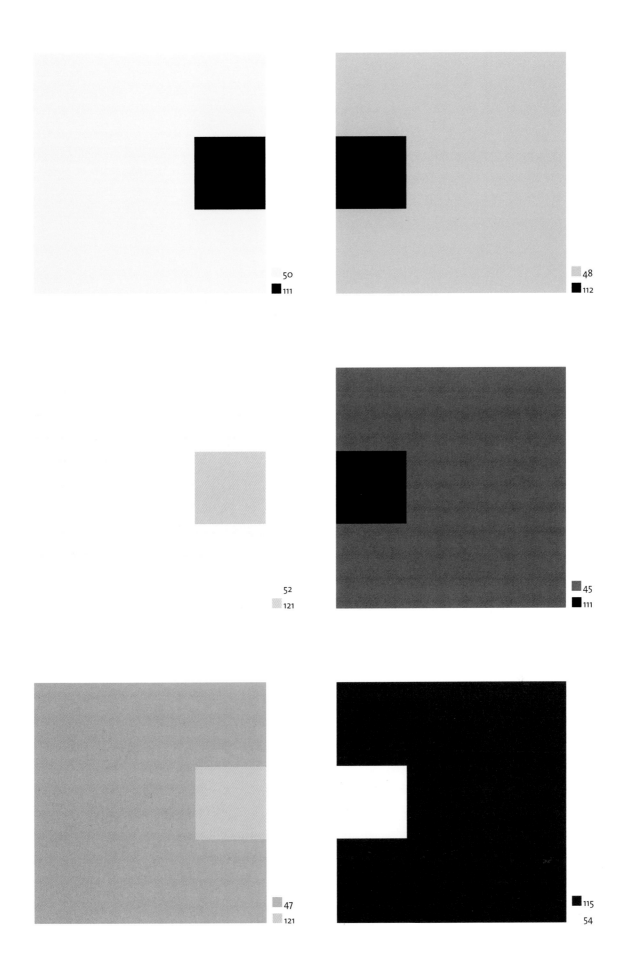

50
111

48
112

52
121

45
111

47
121

115
54

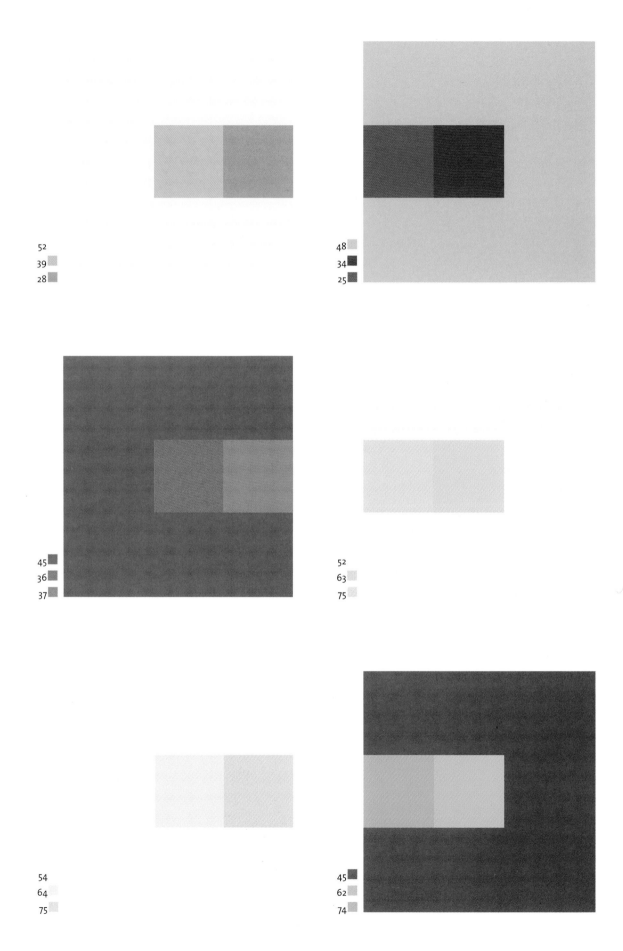

52
39
28

48
34
25

45
36
37

52
63
75

54
64
75

45
62
74

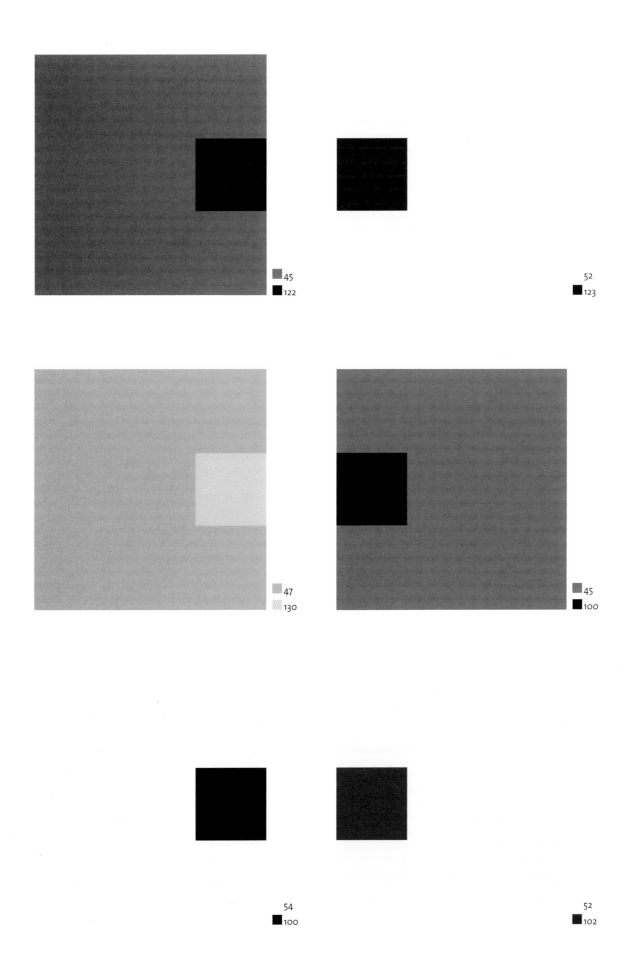

45
122

52
123

47
130

45
100

54
100

52
102

51
133

54
132

53
149

52
148

47
152

46
151

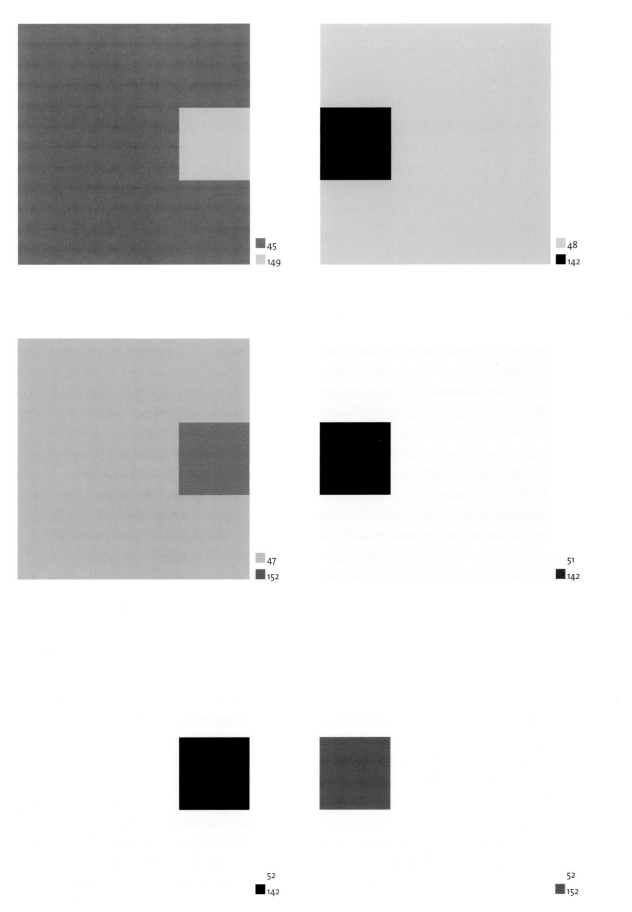

45
149

48
142

47
152

51
142

52
142

52
152

Decorating with a luminescent mix

A luminescent decor captures and reflects the essence of light. From the sun-splashed rays of natural daylight to a thoughtfully placed lamp, the aura of a light-filled room is pleasingly hospitable and filled with the glow of life. Decorate with yellow and its various tints and shades for a home that is always gracious and warm.

The play of natural daylight is the focal point of this symmetrically balanced traditional decor. Butter tinted creams and yellowy sage pair with rich woods and black accents for a welcoming yet formal room.

Luminescent **Tips**

•Decorating with mirrors illuminates your home. Hang them strategically to capture the light of glowing candles, sconces, and chandeliers. A Venetian glass mirror is well suited to a luminous interior. An enduring classic, the fashionable Venetian mirror is distinguished by the decorated and etched mirror frame that surrounds the central mirror plate. First designed to demonstrate the art and skill of Venetian glass makers in the 1600s, they were refined in the nineteenth century by the French.

•Arrange pillar candles in front of the fireplace and stagger heights with a variety of candle holders. Select candles in a variety of traditional tones from classic white to beeswax yellow to particularly enhance a luminescent room. Another option is a candelabrum behind or in front of a fireplace screen. Warm your hearth with a woven basket filled with wood, add decorative fireplace tools like a broom, poker, tongs, shovel, and stand.

•Once traded in the ancient markets of the East, prismatic glass beads capture light and add sparkle. Today you can select from an ever-growing variety of accessories that are adorned with tiny, glittering beads, such as beaded lampshades, votives, table cloths, place mats, pillows, and frames—diminutive jewels well suited to a luminescent decor.

•Bring true warmth to a luminescent decor with comforting throws that are equally at home on the sofa, chair, or ottoman. For chilly days and nights, envelop yourself in a lovely cream Angora or camel cashmere throw, switch to lightweight natural cotton in warmer months.

•Replace plain vanilla foyer or dining room light fixtures with an antique or flea-market find. . Use swing lamps on either side of a bed or strategically mount them by a club chair or sofa in the living room for reading light. Picture lamps, recessed lighting in shelves or under cabinetry, and halogen spots all create focal points with light. Install dimmers and low-voltage bulbs to instantly change the aura of a room from coldly stark to warmly glowing.

[ABOVE]
This mirror is positioned to reflect and maximize the radiance of a nearby chandelier.

[RIGHT]
Yellow and green mix to create the sunny disposition of this affable breakfast nook. Use yellow near glass exterior doors and in rooms with plenty of windows for an open, airy and undeniably cordial look.

essentially green

The most beautiful greens mimic nature.

If green were a person, it would probably be a world-renowned peacemaker. Gentle on the eye, whether it's deep, dark forest green, or the palest lime, green is a color most of us can introduce without creating a color war within our walls. In fact it works well with nearly every color on the color wheel, and can, by its honesty and range, be worked into schemes that excite, calm, comfort, and embrace us.

The Green Range
Some shades of green have more blue in them, and these tend to be cooler, richer, and perhaps more suitable to a formal mood. The moss greens, which have more yellow in them, are warmer, and therefore offer more possibilities for a variety of rooms and furniture styles. As you move down into the lighter hues, the pale greens with a hint of blue, for example, and the moss that evolves to pale lime, the door opens for many who may initially shy away from green as a wall color. At its palest point, green can easily be envisioned by most anyone as complementing upholstery or window treatments where various shades of green mingle with rich or not-so-rich colors. It becomes a soft background that can echo a theme, quietly.

Bringing Green Into the Scene
Green gives you the base to create or support many themes. Here are a few ideas:

• Go country: A home with a casual atmosphere might come into its own with grass or apple greens, the tones with more yellow in them. A country-style kitchen works well with either shade on the walls, the cabinets, or the floor. Painting the floor in a high-gloss green, or covering it with stone or tile with a green tint, keeps the nature theme and frees you to accent with other warm, countryside colors like red or orange. A warm, terra-cotta color floor would also work well here.

• Make a bathroom feel like a spa: The most soothing form of green is the lightest, and whether you choose a blue-green or pale lime, either will hold the calm you desire. Accent with deeper, richer towels if you like, or complementary pale colors such as sand, chocolate brown, pale yellow, peach, blue, or white.

• Bring the outside in: Whether you live in Hawaii or Paris, bringing the outside in via an all-natural palette makes a space pleasing, relaxing, and easy on the eye. Consider giving green the lead in a sunroom, living room, or study—especially if these rooms have outdoor views. That way, the palettes can dovetail, and further support the visual illusion! Use dark, blue-greens to richen the room and enhance the coziness, or lighter hues with complex, multicolored prints that recall spring.

Green Combinations
Remember, you can also have all of these together if you want—it's just a matter of balance. You may find a fabric, for example, that incorporates all these colors, and launch the décor from there with appropriate wall color and window treatment choices.
• Green and red
• Green and yellow
• Green and blue
• Green and orange

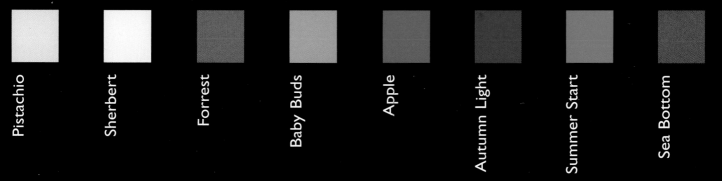

Pistachio · Sherbert · Forrest · Baby Buds · Apple · Autumn Light · Summer Start · Sea Bottom

If you truly love green, this room shows
you how to make it work with different
fabrics, tones, and complements.

Yellow and dark green provide a pleasing combination in this country-style kitchen, and keeping the light color on the walls works especially well with the natural light. The dark green background works well to show off the yellow dishes and knickknacks.

KELLY HOPPEN,

A LONDON-BASED INTERIOR DESIGNER:

"As for green, I used to use a lot of this with black, the dark racing green, and celadon as an accent."

LAURA BOHN,

A NEW YORK–BASED INTERIOR DESIGNER:

"My favorite color is green, green, and green —all shades except forest, ivy, or kelly; lime is okay. Green is the most soothing, and I see it as a neutral because I can put any kind of wood or color on top of it. It really looks great if you mix it with blue and yellow. And, it totally relates to nature."

MINNESOTA-BASED ARCHITECT

KATHERINE HILLBRAND:

"I love greens and purples. I think of green in certain ways though. I'm not an emerald-green person. I like dusty greens, and I think that has to do with being in the woods and the shadows. I'm drawn to an emotional love of trees, so it's primeval. And I do believe in genetic memory, and believe my history had something to do with the forest."

**ALEXANDRA STODDARD,
A NEW YORK-BASED INTERIOR DESIGNER:**

"It would be hard for me to think of a room without having green in it. Interior environments are supposed to echo nature. And blue is the most prevalent in our universe because of the sky! Often, I paint ceilings blue, walls pale green with white trim, or pale yellow walls with white trim. And if I wanted to echo the sunset, I would paint the walls pale pink, and the ceiling pale green."

**BOSTON-BASED INTERIOR DESIGNER
CHARLES SPADA:**

"I think if you want a really beautiful green, go walk through a dappled forest in June and look at the moss in the sunlight, and the shade. There's a palette [beyond] compare! I think its crazy to depend on paint companies to come up with color schemes; you should come up with your own colors."

**NIK RANDALL, AN ARCHITECT WITH BROOKS
STACEY RANDALL, LONDON:**

"I do not think of colors so much in terms of preferring yellows to greens for example, but rather about how a color or series of colors can work with a space to enhance the architecture."

The strategy here was to bring the outside in—or merge the views, green on green. You can do the same with wall paint, wallpaper, or tile, building on texture and variety many ways.

Notice how these pale, mint-green
walls allow the architectural details
of this minimalist-styled room to shine
through. This would work in any room
where you want peace and color quiet.

Tropical

Discover free-spirited tropical style and its brightest spark—outspoken lime green. Exuberant, effervescent, modern, and new, these yellow-enriched greens rejuvenate. The most carefree color of the traditional color wheel, chartreuse brings dynamic energy to any decor. This playful hue has a unique tendency to fall in and out of fashion; however, in a tropical setting this novel color retains its youthful strength, remaining current and crisp. Blend vivid chartreuse with an infusion of citrus-based hues, such as tangerine, shocking pink, and saturated yellow. Pair lilac with lime for a cooling combination. Flatter yellow-greens with natural colors like white, taupe, and rich chocolate hues. Spicy cinnabar and seasoned orange combine to bring heat to the freshest decorating color of the Pacific East.

A symphony of island-inspired materials, such as rattan, bamboo, hemp, and unpolished stone, merge and weave to construct a tropical decor. Fuse low, oversized furnishings and colonial-inspired antiques with Pacific island artifacts, darkly waxed woods, wicker accents, Asian-influenced batiks, embroidered silks, and primitive modern art. Use screens of translucent rice paper or carved wood to divide great rooms. Invite the outdoors in; leave windows unadorned to celebrate the semi-outdoor lifestyle of the islands or appoint with extra-wide 3- to 4-inch.plantation shutters. To recreate the ambiance of a breezy verandah, mass potted tropical plants with infinite variations of fresh yellow greens.

[ABOVE]
Robin's-egg blue walls and magenta window treatments work together to heighten the rousing effect of chartreuse bedding, an Ottoman, and bedside chair. Sizable windowsills hold interior planters that are filled with flowers, beckoning the outdoors into the room. Two sconces illuminate a single framed print of a tropical flower.

[RIGHT]
This sophisticated room is filled with natural materials setting the pace for an unfettered tropical mood. A shallow bowl of pears, bleached wicker, modern mahogany, black lacquer accents, plenty of white and a dash of lime give this room its chic attitude.

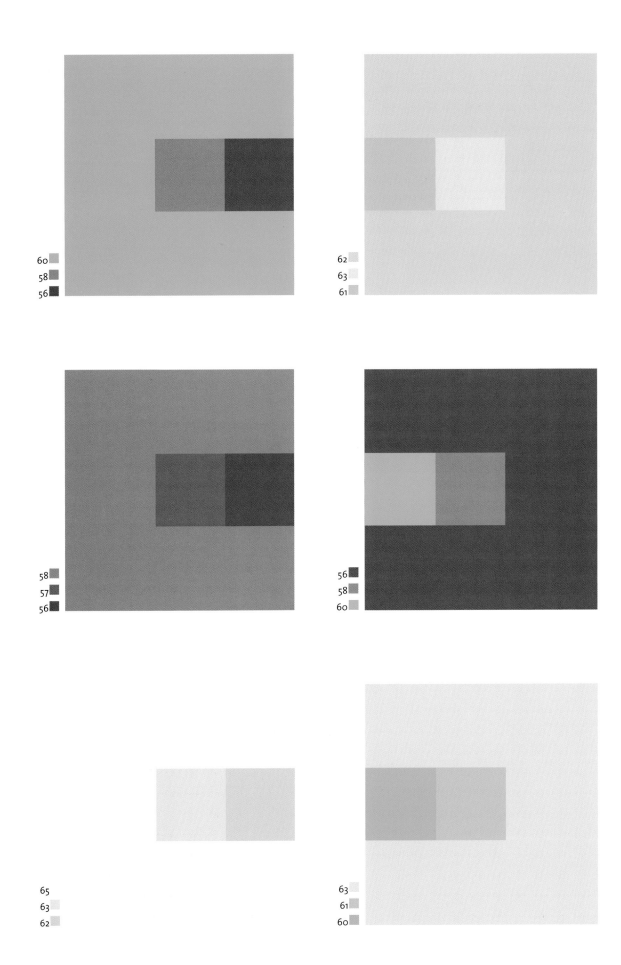

60

58

56

62

63

61

58

57

56

56

58

60

65

63

62

63

61

60

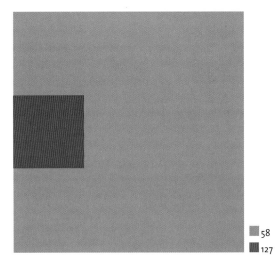

60
122

58
127

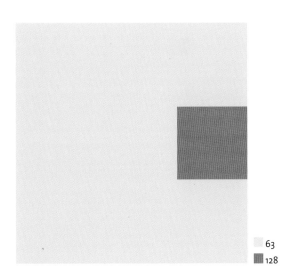

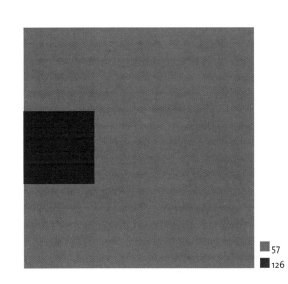

63
128

57
126

61
127

65
131

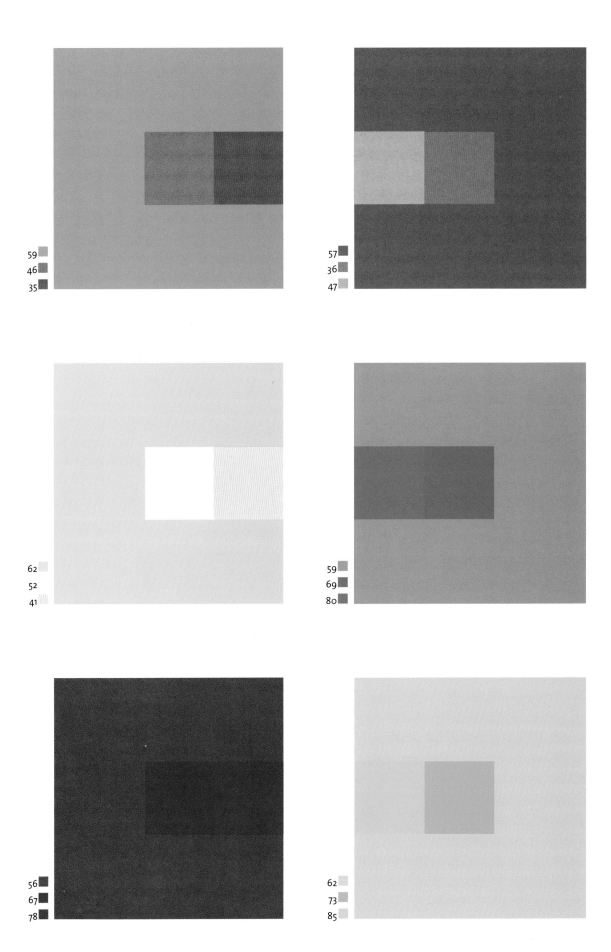

59
46
35

57
36
47

62
52
41

59
69
80

56
67
78

62
73
85

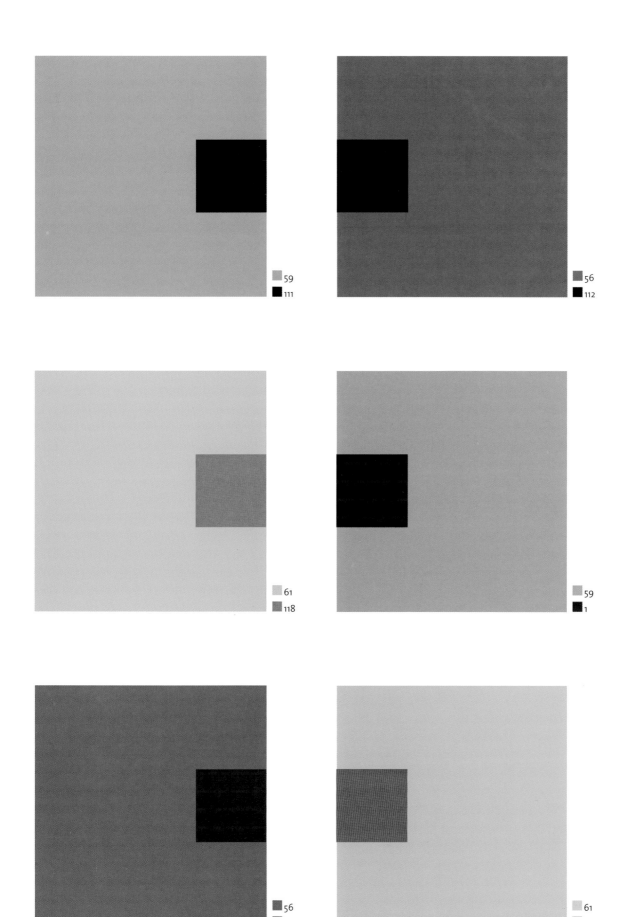

59
111

56
112

61
118

59
1

56
2

61
6

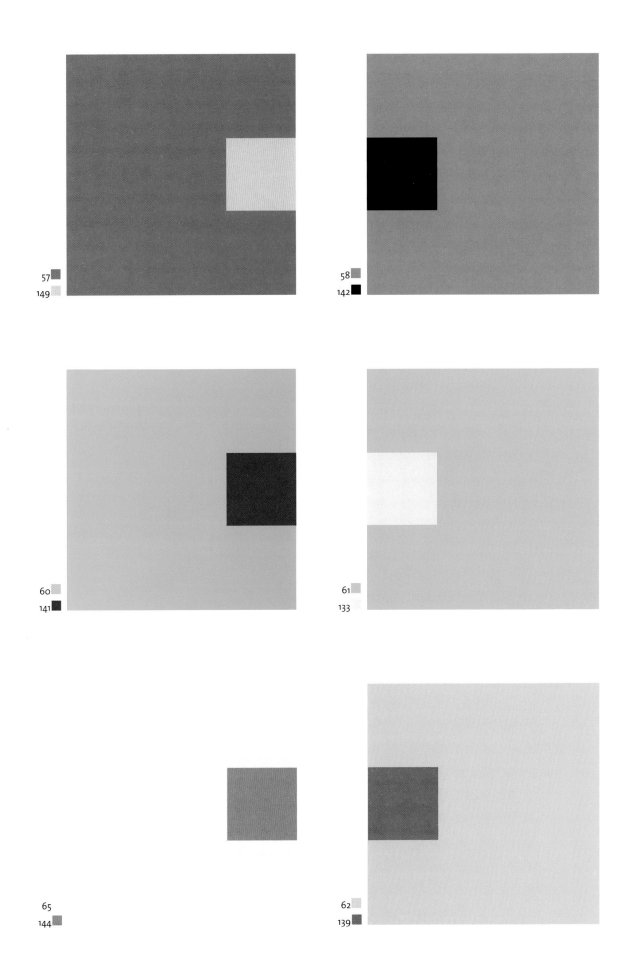

57
149

58
142

60
141

61
133

65
144

62
139

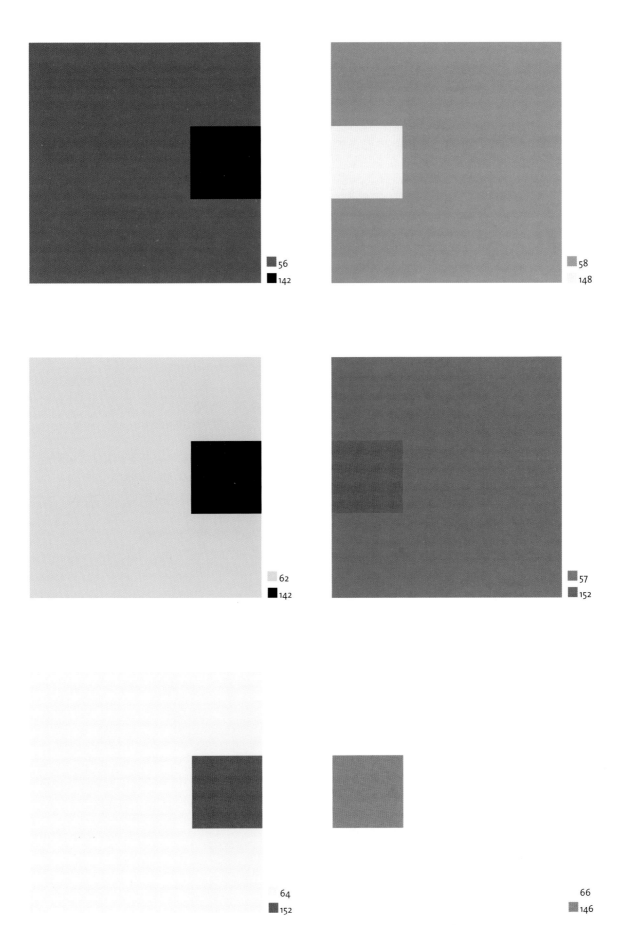

56
142

58
148

62
142

57
152

64
152

66
146

Decorating with a tropical mix

You may hear the call of island life when decorating with the tropics in mind. A tropical palette can be motivating and might herald a change toward a lifestyle that embraces semi-outdoor living. A tropical decor is equally at home with sleek, streamlined modern furnishings or traditional dark wood antiques. Tropical hues blend with other saturated hues, such as vivid magenta, spicy orange, and lemon yellow. The vibrant colors of a tropical color scheme work well with the deepest colors of the outdoors. Imagine deep forest greens, peaty dark browns, and evening-sky blues.

With pared-down furnishings, and greens as fresh and vibrant as palm fronds, this modern interior keeps the mood breezy and tropical.

Tropical **Tips**

•Plant caladiums (an easy-to-grow annual tropical bulb) or low maintenance ornamental grasses, such as bamboo or pampas, outside windows for big, bold views of a tropical garden. Or simply place natural elements—perhaps an orchid spray—in front of a window to create a visual connection to the exterior view.

•Reconfigure a porch, sunroom, or large living area for semi-outdoor living by installing ceiling fans, screens, and natural stone floors that will weather. Outfit garden-style furnishings with weather-resistant cushions and pillows.

•At the end of your bed place a teak bench or lacquer chest, and add a thick cushion. Use this bedside nook to display extra pillows or blankets in chartreuse and complementary hues of vivid magenta.

•Consider positioning a bed in an unexpected area of the bedroom. Push a twin or full bed against a wall and pile it with pillows for a cozy day bed. Angle it toward the door or place directly in front of a vibrantly curtained window to create the illusion of an exterior view as a "headboard". To add drama to the "headboard" effect, select drapes in saturated hues of citrus such as lime, lemon or tangerine. As evening falls, shutter the window or pull down inexpensive bamboo blinds for privacy.

•Display travel-inspired collectibles, such as globes and outdated maps of exotic lands and faraway places in bamboo and dark wood frames. Position a standing electrical fan in black or stainless steel on a side table or atop a stack of travel books to provide gentle, "tropical" breezes in any room.

[ABOVE]
A generous arrangement of freshly cut flowers in citrus shades makes a lush arrangement that's brimming with tropical abundance.

[RIGHT]
Exuberant and modern yellow-enriched greens rejuvenate. Match them up to create a youthful and restorative dreaming space.

Tranquil

To connect with the tranquil outdoors and compose a home filled with peaceful serenity, use green—the color of life. Look to the living outdoors to find an infinite palette of greens from which to select, from youthful spring green to the intriguingly ancient colors of richly aged verdigris. Create a historical mood by deepening almost any green—leaf green, grass green, lettuce green, forest green. Achieve the eternal aura of an ancient forest by decorating with cast iron, carved stone, and garden statuary. Add a multitude of yellows from saffron to lemon for a sundappled blend. White and cream are two plain partners for green that soften and soothe. Energize the tranquil properties of fertile green with its most natural companion, earthen red. In addition, brown and gray blend and pair well with green. To link your home interior with the outdoors, there is no better color than green.

Alive and cooling, a tranquil palette brings the outdoors in. Discover that nothing brings new life to tired furnishings more than a color scheme that revolves around green. Mix spirited greens with pale woods to give the light and free feeling of summer; partner darkened greens with deep, rich woods such as walnut and mahogany for a mood of tranquil solitude. Bring outdoor furnishings in—use outdoor planters, fold-up furniture, plant stands, wooden folding tables, worn wicker, bamboo, bentwood pieces, director's chairs, hand-me-downs and other discards. Combine these new-found treasures with floral cottons, needlepoint or crewel pillows, and traditional "awning-striped" canvas cushions. Finally, begin to cultivate decorative elements such as a fascinating terrarium or two for decor that will evolve much like your own garden.

[ABOVE]
An old painted bench serves as a lengthy coffee table in this tranquil, sun-splashed room. Plenty of cozy seating, pillows, and throws add to the comforting atmospherics. Note that the cushions are ever-so-slightly faded, and the worn furnishings have lovingly stood the test of time.

[RIGHT]
Arrange simple clay pots right on your kitchen counter if you don't have a windowsill. Paint tired wooden kitchen cabinets a cooling green to emulate a greenhouse environment.

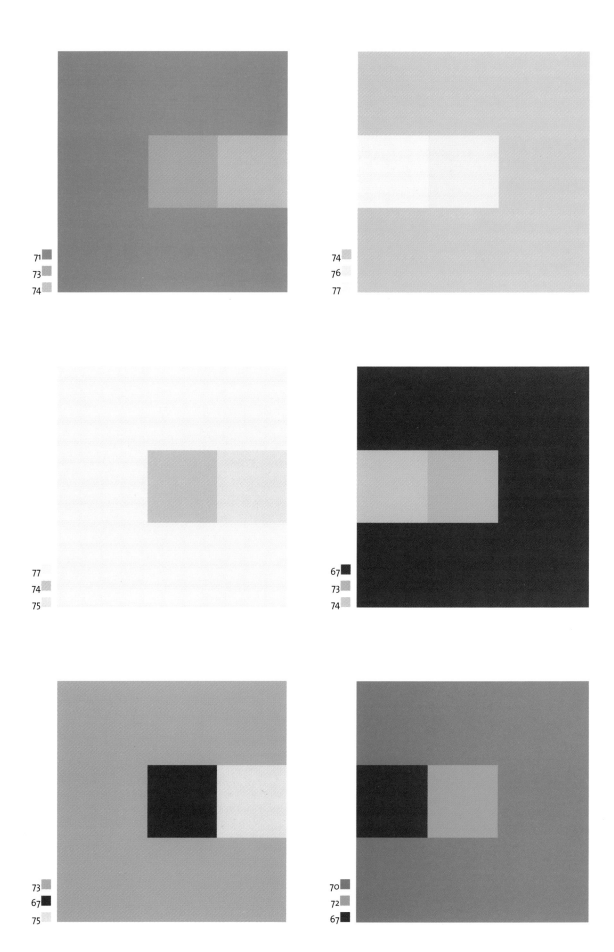

71
73
74

74
76
77

77
74
75

67
73
74

73
67
75

70
72
67

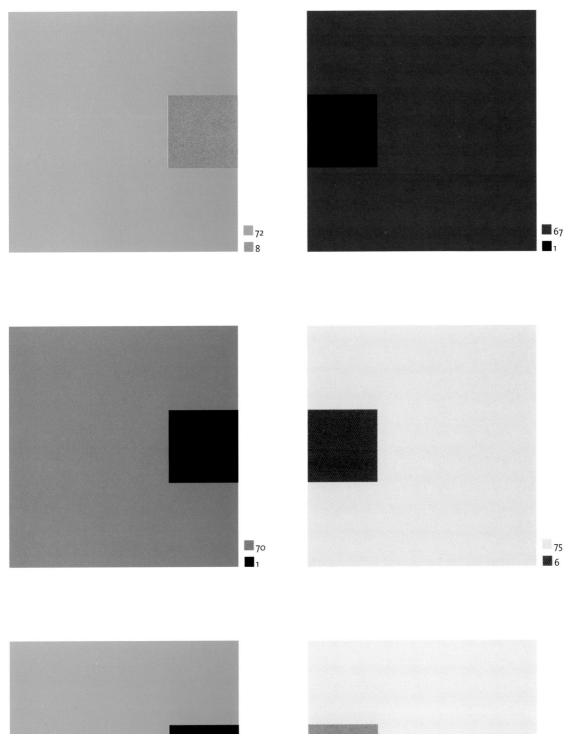

72
8

67
1

70
1

75
6

72
3

76
8

52
39
28

48
34
25

45
36
37

52
63
75

54
64
75

45
62
74

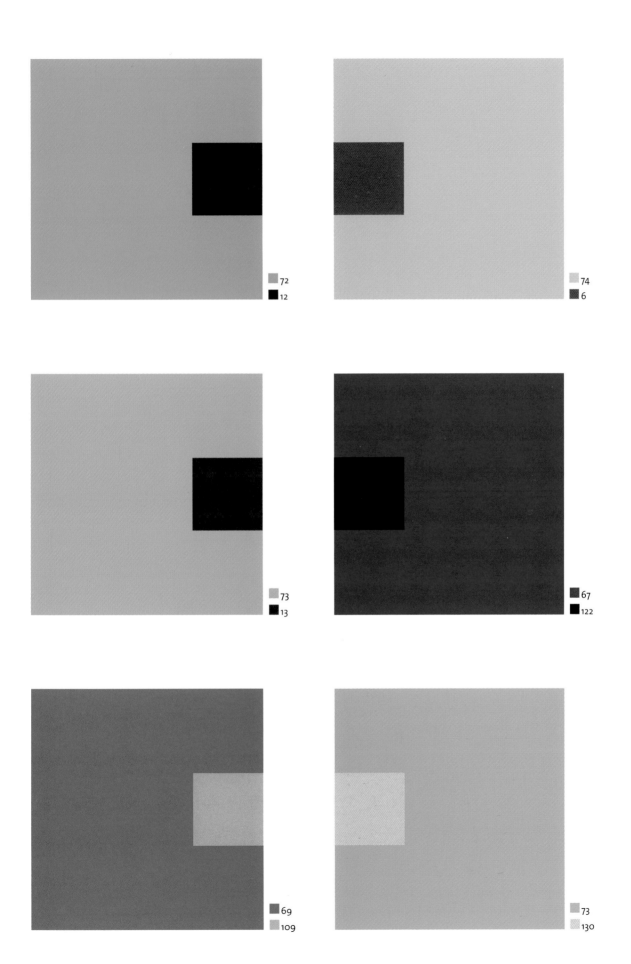

72
12

74
6

73
13

67
122

69
109

73
130

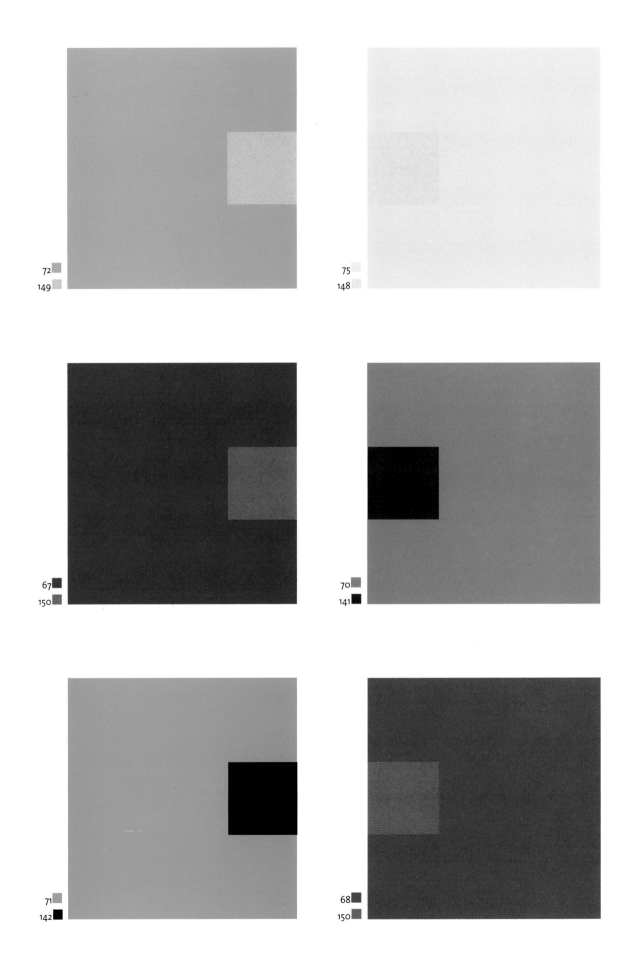

72
149

75
148

67
150

70
141

71
142

68
150

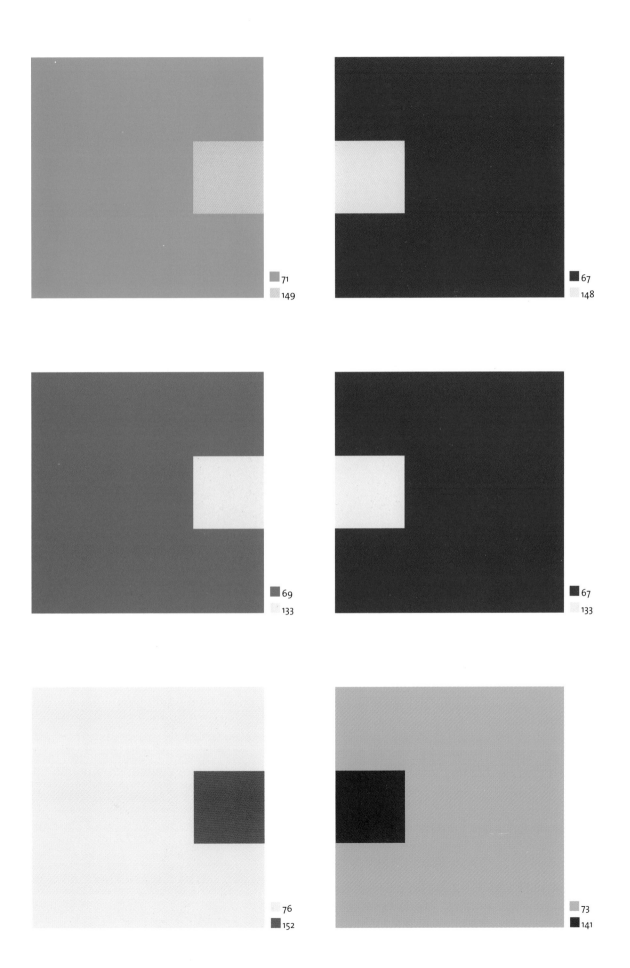

71
149

67
148

69
133

67
133

76
152

73
141

Decorating with a tranquil mix

Tranquil interiors are mood enhancing and nurturing. A cool palette will blend comfortably with a wide assortment of furnishings and often feature a variety of greens, one of nature's most abundant, peaceful colors. Red, the most stimulating color, is green's color wheel opposite. When used sparingly, a bit of red will bring interest and energy to a tranquil color scheme.

A room needn't be flooded with light to create a tranquil garden mood. Mix seasonal plants like these daisies with hardy indoor varieties. Highlighting an exposed brick wall or mural adds to the indoor garden atmosphere.

Tranquil **Tips**

•You don't need to own a conservatory or greenhouse to create a garden environment. Maintain the mood of your tranquil interior by selecting indoor plants that reflect the seasons. Throughout summer, feature potted plants such as hydrangeas, begonias, impatiens, and periwinkle. For autumn, pot ornamental kale; in early winter, fashion branches with berry clusters into sparse wreaths; anticipate early spring by planting bulbs such as amaryllis, crocus, and hyacinth.

•If the room you are decorating is accessible to an outdoor garden, select a floor covering that's durable and easy to clean, such as laminated wood or oversized tile. Select from warm woods and stone floor coverings with a hint of red (the complement of green) to bring a rich, rustic undertone to a tranquil environment.

•While a chandelier lends romance to a garden-inspired environment, it may not be practical. A ceiling fan is a functional choice when cooling is critical. Add a light kit and install a dimmer for controlled overhead lighting.

•Take inventory of your current possessions and tap into your own indoor garden style. Random purchases, family keepsakes, even questionable college acquisitions, can have a second life when painted, restored, re-covered, or recycled with various tints and shades of peaceful green.

•Display vintage bird and botanical prints, accumulated belongings from travels, antique wooden farm tools, or perch a row of bird houses atop a mantel.

•Salvage and reclaim a collection of containers—from coffee cups to odd glassware—to accommodate a kitchen herb garden beside a sunny window.

•Consider investing in a classic solid teak bench, occasional table, ottoman, or chaise lounge. Beautiful indoors and out, teak is a durable, weather-resistant wood. To achieve a silvery gray patina that will pair beautifully with garden green, simply leave the furniture outdoors to age.

[ABOVE]
A grouping of assorted terra-cotta pots planted with artichokes, white flowers, moss, and cabbage with candles nestled inside makes an unstudied centerpiece for a casual gathering.

[RIGHT]
Create an indoor shrine to the outdoors using natural materials, such as bamboo, stones, and plants, for the perfect place to find peace.

primarily blue

Blue walls become exquisite trimmed with pearl white: subtle accents of black in picture frames and furnishings sugges a stylish, French influence.

Blue is one of those ubiquitous colors that, once you look for it, you are bound to find it somewhere in most homes. It could be a tiny dash subtly woven into a patterned rug, or in the bright blue sky of a painting, but it's there somewhere! Like red, in its deepest, darkest tone, blue is a big color, and it makes a statement. But unlike red, it's a statement that is easier to manipulate. Perhaps you've ignored blue—thought it only works with a certain furnishing style, or that it's confining. Let go of those notions! Think of blue as a color that can add depth to your home's palette.

The Blue Range

The densest version of blue is midnight, and moving a few spaces from that on the color wheel is blue with a bit more red in it. Both are dramatic and as strong in attitude as red. We commonly see these versions of blue in dressier, elegant spaces where dark woods prevail and the mood is well defined by accessories. These hues are literally light years in mood from paler versions like baby blue or the green-blue robin's egg blue. The latter can come into your design scheme in fabrics with a floral motif, where contrast plays hard, or through subdued monotone silks that can set the stage for the sublime. Dark blues give you a backdrop that can enrich a simple room or echo the lushness of a high-in-detail, architecturally complex room. Move down the light scale and you create space that sings spring or spa.

Bringing Blue Into the Scene

Following are some ways to bring varying shades of blue into your home palette.

Light Blues

Blue has a reputation for being soothing, calm, and sometimes cool. Choose the palest blue hue that appeals to you, and bring it into a room where those qualities matter. Using blue in its palest form gives you the latitude to accent it with other colors you normally migrate toward. The blue-green tones are reminiscent of the island environments and spas, and work well in bathroom, sunroom, or bedroom. Pinks, yellows, oranges, and like hues can be added to complement and hold the theme. Choose pale blues with red tones and you work up a richer palette with shades of red or gold. Remember, you don't have to make a big color commitment, such as with gold furnishings or fabric. It can be as simple as accents via art in gold frames.

Deep Blues

Think cobalt or midnight blue to make a statement and anchor a distinct mood in a space. Imagine your dining room painted with a high-gloss or lacquered midnight blue effect-set against a rich mahogany wainscoting. Keep the ceiling white and you've created an elegant cocoon that will glow with candlelight. If the thought of your living room in either of these shades seems over the top, consider bringing them in if only for the window treatment. Imagine a yellow-on-the-verge-of-gold wall with rich, midnight-blue brocade drapes. Another way to introduce dark blue is through your bedding. Imagine off-white bedroom walls encircling a cobalt blue comforter—pillows piled high with a warm or cool palette with deep blue accents.

Blue Combinations

Remember the color translates the mood when considering combinations. Play with versions of light and dark, warm and cool to find the look that pleases you most:
• Blue and gold • Blue and yellow
• Blue and red • Blue and orange
• Blue and green

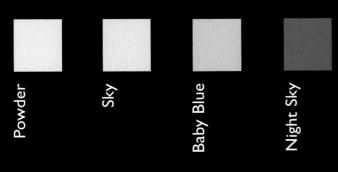

Powder

Sky

Baby Blue

Night Sky

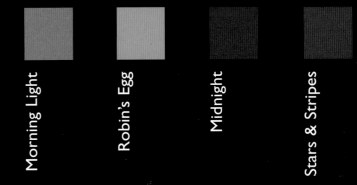

Morning Light

Robin's Egg

Midnight

Stars & Stripes

Kitchens don't always have to be energized and hot. Here a pale blue kitchen with light blond wood makes for a serene workplace.

Before you paint, think about the views from one room into another. Here a bright-blue dining room looks into a bright-green library—the pleasant change and contrast easily leads the eye from one place to another.

**ALEXANDRA STODDARD,
A NEW YORK—BASED INTERIOR DESIGNER:**

"I like to have blue in my home because of the sky, and water, green because of the land, and yellow because of the sun...all the colors that I love for my work are inspired by nature. In one way or another I try to bring these nature references to where we live because I think we are starved for them!"

**NEW YORK–BASED INTERIOR DESIGNER
ZINA GLAZEBROOK:**

"I've chosen to live near the water so the palette I respond to comes from sand, the colors of beach stones and shells, the ocean's blue grays.... I find blue [to be] elegant."

**PARIS–BASED INTERIOR DESIGNER
ERIC SCHMITT:**

"I generally use raw white for the skin of the house. I also use pure white in isolated places to add light. I like strong color in very bright rooms; I generally use rather dark and strong shades like China red or slate blue."

JEFFREY BILHUBER,

A NEW YORK–BASED INTERIOR DESIGNER:

"We always do an icy, frosty version of blue in a bedroom. Most people say they want a warm pink or yellow, but those colors work in the complete reverse because you will look blue in rooms that color. If you use blue in the room, it brings out your color as warm skin tones. Test this by holding your hand up to a cool color and see how your skin looks!"

CHARLES SPADA,

A BOSTON–BASED INTERIOR DESIGNER:

"If I'm talking to a woman client about color, I notice what colors she wears. We're hoping to do this new apartment and the owner wears the most beautiful soft colors. Her favorite is green—blue, and I want to pick that for her [home] because it works with her skin tone and eyes."

WASHINGTON, D.C.–BASED INTERIOR

DESIGNER, MARY DOUGLAS DRYSDALE:

"I think there's a resurgence in the use of color. Why? Because there is a certain sort of dullness that sets in and people get tired of seeing the same old same old."

Periwinkle walls, in combination with bare windows, welcomes the blue of the sky and natural light in this peaceful bedroom. With barely another color in the room, it holds its Zen qualities.

Here is a room that exemplifies the benefits of bringing just the right blue and yellow together in a theme. Tossing the yellow pillows across the sea of a blue couch is a great touch, and the island of green and yellow in the foreground adds yet another element of color interest in the space. Notice, too, how the neutral walls make the fabric the star.

Consider giving family photos, dressed in rich gold frames, a solid color anchor of blue.

NEW YORK–BASED INTERIOR DESIGNER ZINA GLAZEBROOK:

"I think we all have an indigenous sense of color, and that comes from our geography—where we grew up in nature's palette, and what we sought out (geography—wise) as adults. I also think color has a phase quality to it, like fashion forecasting, and I think you go through phases too."

CHRIS CASSON MADDEN, DESIGNER, AUTHOR, AND HGTV HOST:

"One way for people to get into color without going whole hog is with wallpaper. I think I was afraid of it before, and now if I want to make a statement, [I find] it allows me to in different ways."

MINNESOTA–BASED ARCHITECT KATHERINE HILLBRAND:

"The building gives you feedback. A lot of people may think they want a blue room, but it isn't until the form of the house evolves that you can decide that. I feel experimenting with color is a good idea. Some people are afraid to paint a wall. My feeling is you should paint it, and then paint it again if it's wrong. That's the joy of paint."

Coastal

Coastal colors not only refresh and invigorate, these hues originating in air and water are positively buoyant and restorative.
From watery pale aquamarine to the dark blue-green of a stormy sea, these cooling hues are traditionally used in oceanside decor. Seek the colors of this palette for their renewing properties. A variety of ultramarine hues are rejuvenating, uplifting, crisp, clean and ever-popular for the bath and bedroom.

Pair watery seascape hues with driftwood silvery grays, cooling whites, and grayed blues for a marine-inspired decor that also adds restraint. Mix with true blues, navy, and emerald green for an analogous approach. Touches of complementary coral and sandy orange will enhance and give complexity to this soulful color scheme that is never quite out of fashion.

Coastal colors are easy on the eye and a breeze to use when decorating. They appear to blend and recede much as the tide. For fabrics that inspire coastal living, select from bold stripes, cotton duck, hard-wearing terry cloth, and simple checks. Tiles in various shades, thickly bound sisal, nautical accents, as well as a variety of furniture styles serve the colors of the sea well. With this palette it is easy to create an informal attitude, casual and light—your own fusion of sea and sand and sky.

[ABOVE]
Mix and match an assortment of linens for the bed, bath, and kitchen, such as this light and airy stack of white, yellow, and blue-green patterned sheets, coverlets, and bedding.

[RIGHT]
Multi-colored tiles with slight variations in color in the bath evoke the soothing mood of the sea just as the marlin mosaic reflects its energy. Try an assortment of tile sizes and shapes for a flowing, rhythmic effect.

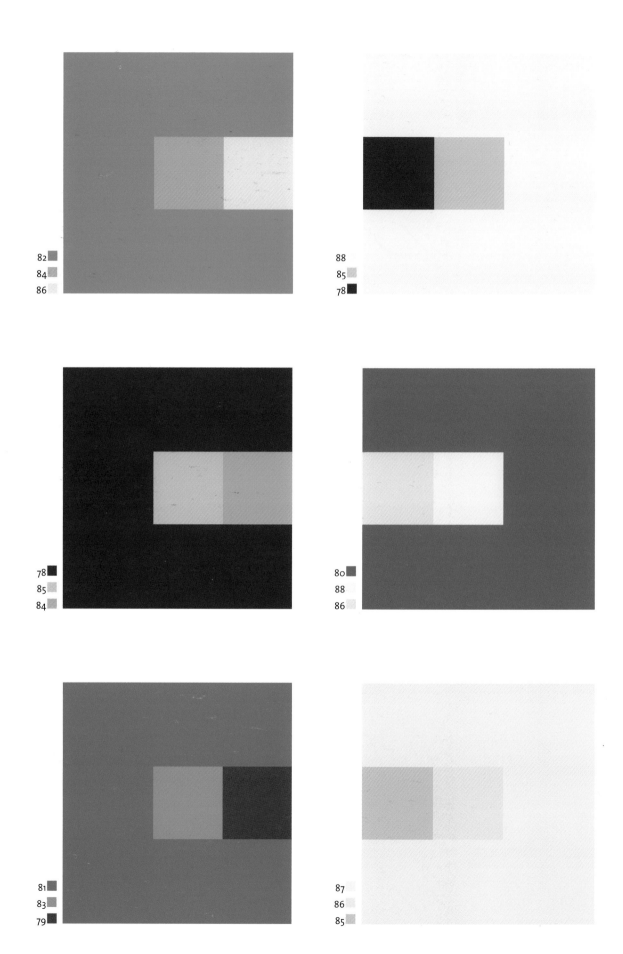

82
84
86

88
85
78

78
85
84

80
88
86

81
83
79

87
86
85

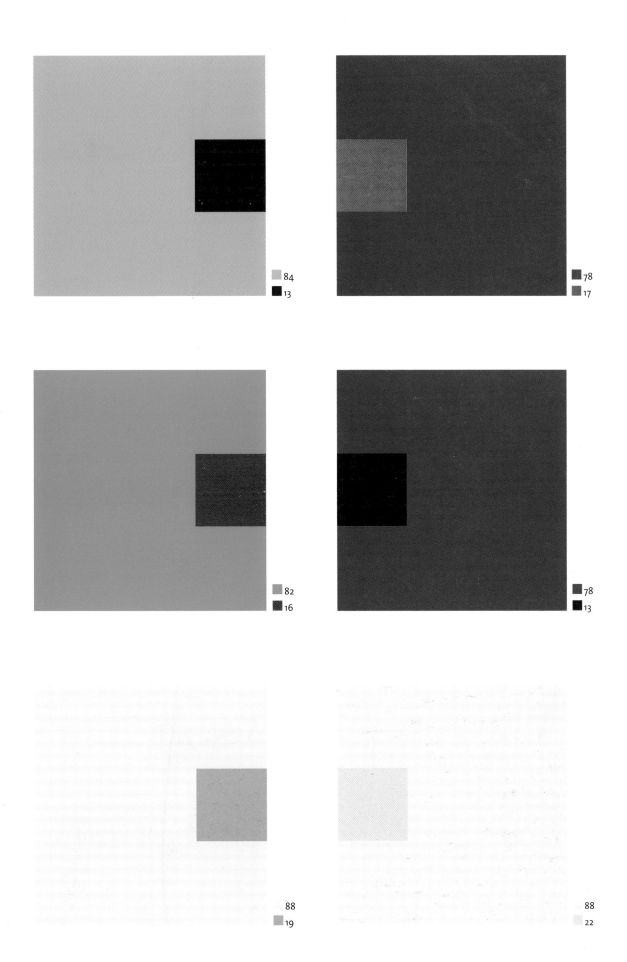

84
13

78
17

82
16

78
13

88
19

88
22

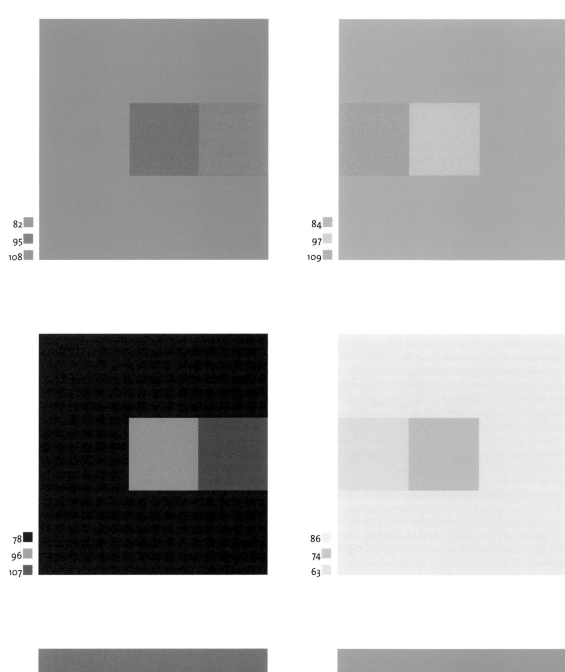

82
95
108

84
97
109

78
96
107

86
74
63

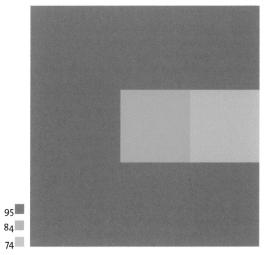

95
84
74

83
110
99

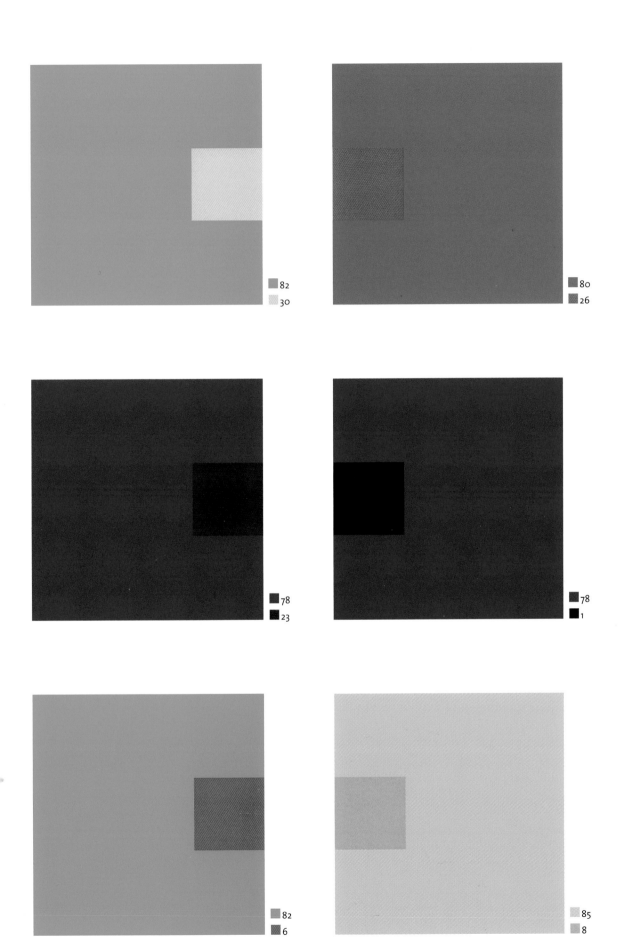

82
30

80
26

78
23

78
1

82
6

85
8

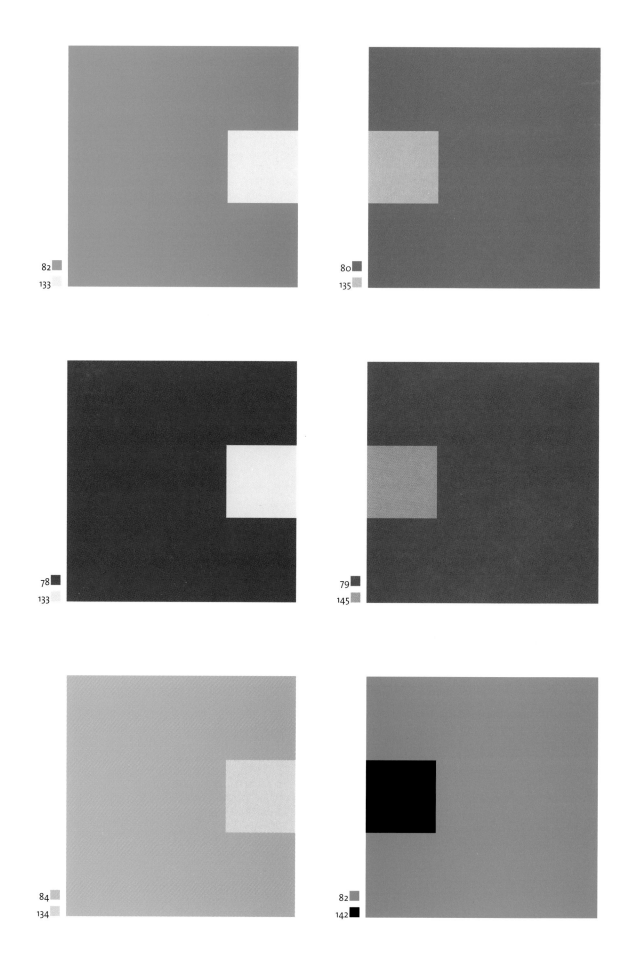

82

133

80

135

78

133

79

145

84

134

82

142

81
146

78
145

79
149

81
152

85
149

86
150

Decorating with
a coastal mix

A coastal palette is transforming and cooling.

Impressionistic hues and ever-changing coastal

colors alternately stir the spirit and offer a

calming port. This palette can be lightened for

summer and deepened for winter. Its cool tones

bring a quiet, restful mood to any decor.

Pair a coastal mix with antique pine furnishings,

flea-market finds that have been freshly

whitewashed, or contemporary furnishings with

clean lines. Coastal tones blend well with other

planet based colors such as a pearly blue, grass

green, dusky gray, and berry red.

Soft, comfortable bedding featuring aquatic colors with tidal
designs that embody the renewing qualities of a coastal environment. Replenish your soul with nearby books, a journal,
and a sketchpad.

Coastal **Tips**

•Transforming and cooling, the colors of the sea may be the most consistently available and versatile. To avoid the look of perpetual, summer use grays, deep seaweed green, and peaty moss hues for soft furnishings in the winter months. Lighten with translucent watery hues as spring and summer return.

•The catch is not to give in to the cliché of seaside living, with shells and starfish abounding. Think strategically when using nautical accessories: a little can go a long way.

•Think of how you live before you accessorize and anticipate your needs. Places stacks of well-worn novels near the bed, display candles and small luxuries in the bath, hang kitchen dish towels near the sink on homemade shell pegs, and even keep classic board games handy on a coffee or sofa table.

•Mix fabric patterns such as stripes, florals, solids, and checks. The key is to look for one or two common colors such as teal and emerald green that will unite the variety of patterns. Wash your bedding and comforters (over and over and over) for a seaworn coastal look that's lived in, soft, and cozy.

•Paint paneling, bookshelves, storage cabinets, and furniture to achieve a casual, custom look. If your wood floor is old and damaged, consider painting the surface a crisp dove-gray or oyster-white to anchor the luminescent turquoise of the sea.

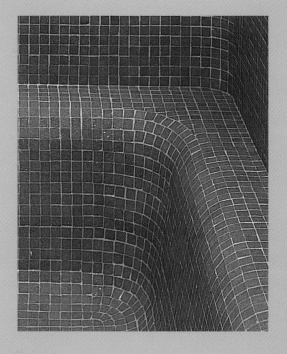

[ABOVE]
Multi-colored tiles with slight variations in color in the bath evoke the soothing mood of the sea. Try an assortment of tile sizes and shapes from small to medium, rectangular and square, for a flowing, rhythmic effect.

[RIGHT]
Create a coastal still life with translucent glassware accents such as a cobalt blue vase and a hand-blown glass pitcher grouped together with bath salts and potions in clear and frosted glass bottles.

Classic

Possibly the most classic color for interiors is blue, a color so beloved it's nearly everyone's favorite hue. More cozy than formal, like an over-stuffed wing chair, blue is the most comfortable classic. Charming and sentimental, classical blue is a time-tested favorite for kitchens, guest rooms, and formal living areas. Blue almost always harmonizes with other blues. Cornflower blue, steely gray blue, and dark navy blue all blend and merge to create the contemplative mood of blue. Mix gentle shades of indigo and lavender to enjoy the nostalgic sweetness so typified by blue. Mix blue with the most luminous color, yellow, for an uplifting, whimsical mood. Enliven a sedate blue with its complement, orange, whose tints and tones restore equilibrium to a blue decor that has gone cold by bringing brilliance and luminosity to this cooling hue.

At its most unpretentious, blue is a work horse. Imagine deep denim and chambray paired with dark waxed woods, fruitwood, or pine. Natural hues like oatmeal, ivory, and nutmeg temper a variety of blues, from dark navy to brilliant sapphire. Simple printed cottons, linens, florals, paisleys, tiny prints, woven jacquard, sheer fabrics, and laces all work nicely with time-treasured blues. Mix with sage greens and berry colors for the mood of an English garden. Warm blue with rosy pinks, reds, and rich brick hues. For furnishings, select cozy sofas, oversized love seats, high four-poster beds, and upholstered ottomans and footstools.

[ABOVE]
Combine classic blue with sage greens, purply blues and creamy oatmeal hues to create a decorating mix that's not only historic but refreshingly modern.

[RIGHT]
A tradition of decoration revolves around the classic combination of blue and white. Select from a variety of English inspired fabric patterns for a room that's both refined and homey.

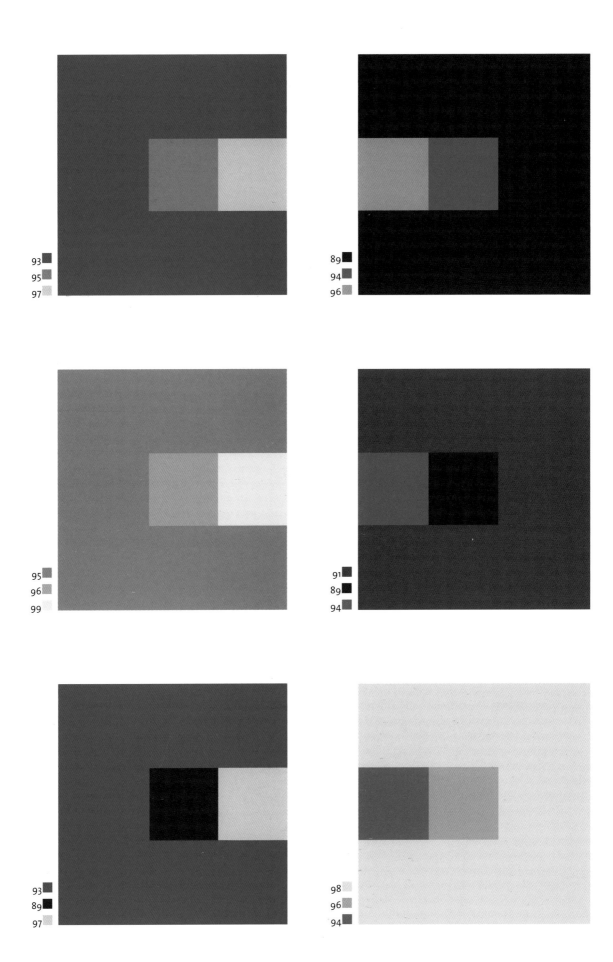

93
95
97

89
94
96

95
96
99

91
89
94

93
89
97

98
96
94

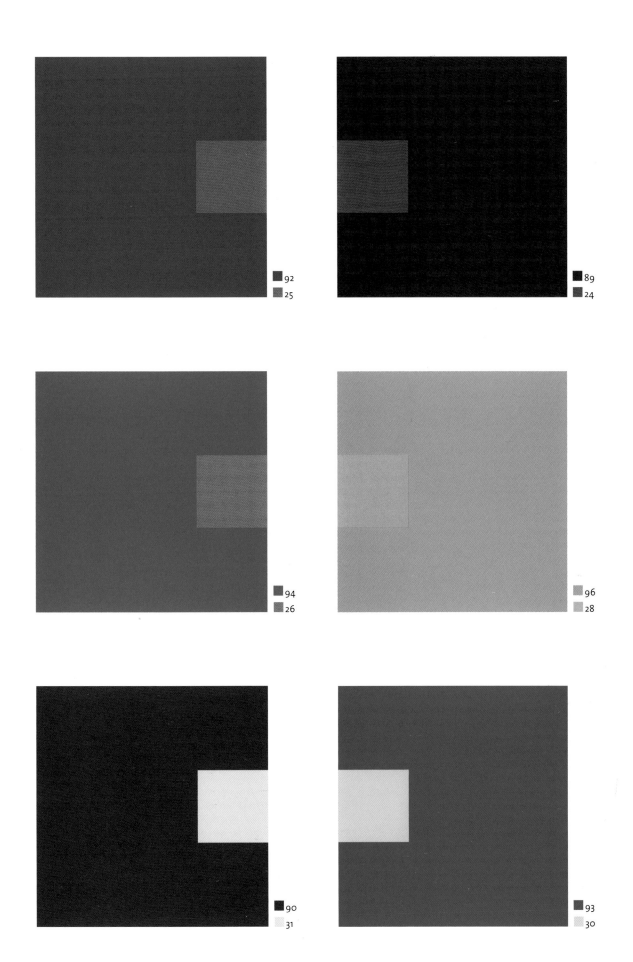

92
25

89
24

94
26

96
28

90
31

93
30

91
112
101

93
103
115

89
106
116

90
105
84

95
109
85

94
82
72

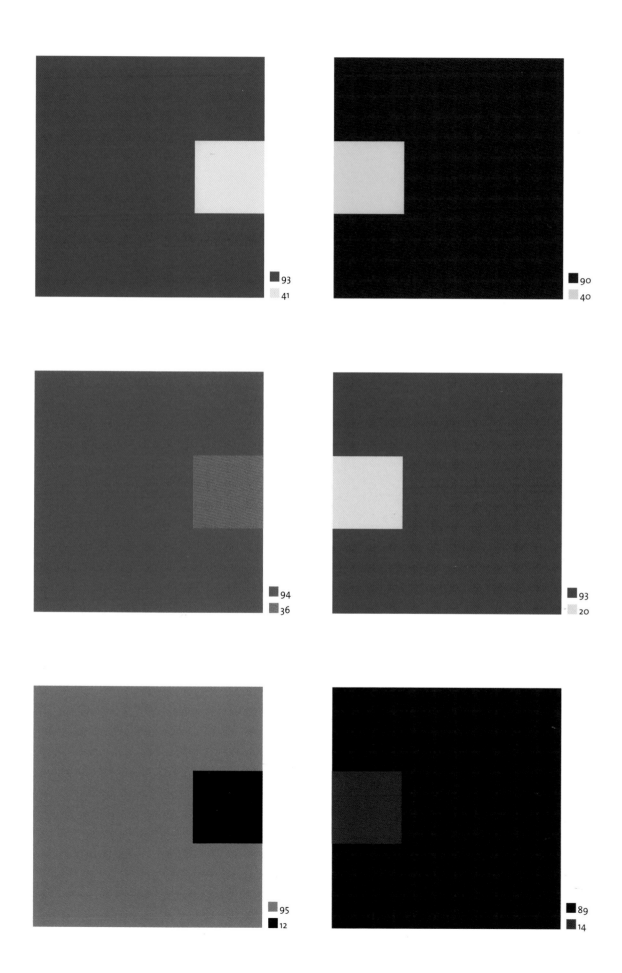

93
41

90
40

94
36

93
20

95
12

89
14

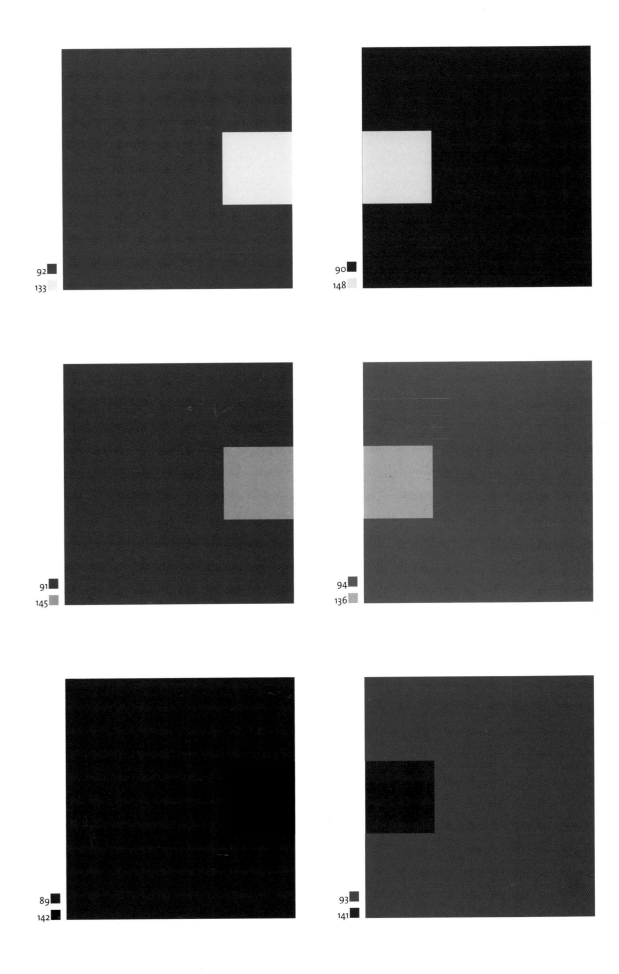

NEUTRAL

92
133

90
148

91
145

94
136

89
142

93
141

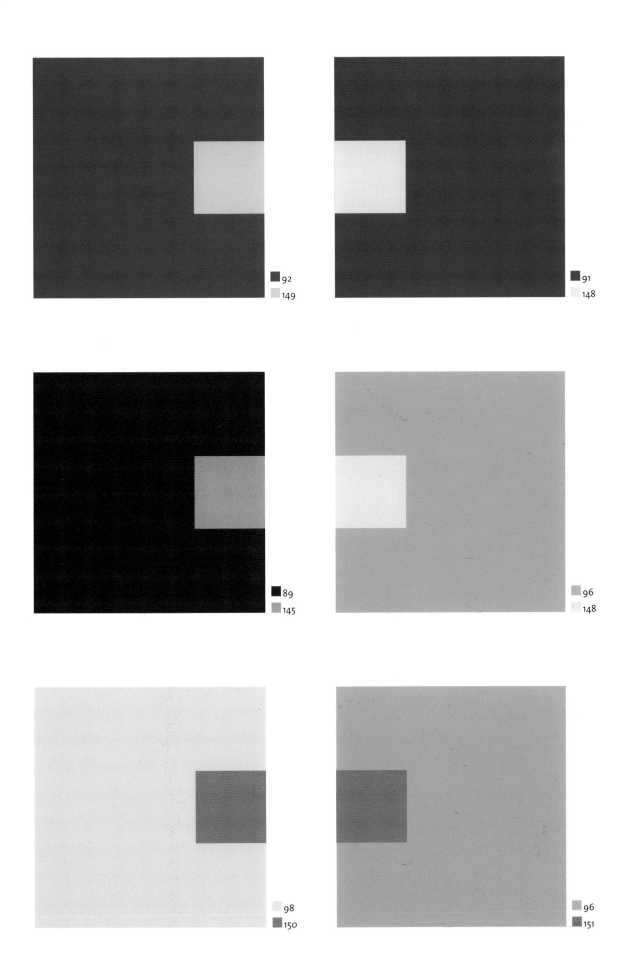

92
149

91
148

89
145

96
148

98
150

96
151

Decorating with
a classic mix

The color of the newest star and as expansive as

the skies, blue emanates visual lightness.

Airy and calm, a blue color scheme is a truly

classic foundation. Blue is the centerpiece of

countless palettes that are at home with a

variety of historically inspired fabrics and

furnishings. Serene and spacious, a room that's

decorated with blue exudes a sense of order and

well being. Lend a bit of history to any space and

decorate with timeless and true blue.

Earth hues surround and heighten traditional blues.
For example, a natural jute rug paired with lightly buffed
terra-cotta walls provides a neutral backdrop for this
blue-centered room.

Classic **Tips**

•Scandinavian decor often employs a dove gray blue to heighten architectural accents. Consider painting trim and moldings a light steel blue. Or paint the ceiling of an interior room or an outside porch a softly muted sky blue. The blue surface will recede to give the illusion of a celestial sky.

•Table lamps add warmth and light to classic decor. In a bedroom, replace old lampshades with pretty printed fabric shades, or use classic creamy solid shades in a living area. Column-style metal bases or simple wood candlesticks make sturdy traditional lamp bases.

•Throughout the ages it has been believed that blue keeps flies away, explaining why it's the most classic color for kitchens. Bring blue to your modern kitchen—arrange and hang a collection of porcelain blue plates with intricate designs and illustrations; display cobalt blue glassware; paint kitchen niches and cabinet interiors a soothing robin's egg blue; or add a tile backsplash of handpainted delft blue tiles. Select stool and chair cushions in blue-based fabrics that feature traditional patterns like cotton gingham, blocky checks, and bold stripes.

•Pile soft sink-in sofas and four-poster beds with wonderfully embellished pillows. Choose classic designs, such as fleur-de-lis, coats of arms, and heraldic motifs. Collect needlepoint and tasseled velvet plush pillows for old-world style.

•Search through discarded wallpaper books and at antique stores and flea markets for botanical, vintage bird, and large-scale floral prints. Frame in gilt, bamboo, or distressed painted frames. To determine placement, first arrange them on the floor and then hang on the wall as a decorative group.

•Many flowers have blooms of blue, such as modest pansies, blue bonnets, and delphinium. Since budding blues are more challenging to find in the winter, try a dried arrangement of silvery blue hydrangeas and lavender. If you prefer a living display, plant masses of lilac blue hyacinths in a shallow bowl for bell-shaped blooms from the chilly season to early spring.

[ABOVE]
A prized collection of china is presented three ways: hung on the wall, stacked in an architectural niche, and casually arranged on a wall shelf for a charming display.

[RIGHT]
Decorate a kitchen with whimsical checks of blue, white and accents of violet.

essentially violet

Experiment with dynamic color combinations in places where they'll be appreciated. Here, a child's bedroom embraces city life, illustrated in bold hues of purple, lilac, blue, and gold.

It seems people either take to violet from the start, and use it confidently, or they just don't ever warm up to it. One reason might be because it is not commonly used, so none of us has a lot of exposure to it. Often, violet enters design schemes quietly as supplements to fabric patterns or as a punctuation point in rooms—big, satiny pillows strung across a contemporary couch, as regal, flowing velvet drapes, or as a single purple chair that makes a statement. If you're on the fence about violet, consider this chapter as a place to get a new view. Perhaps you will be inspired to try it in a room that needs a color boost and a dash of drama.

The Violet Range

In its darkest form, violet is dramatic, moody, and a natural for rooms where formality reigns—deep purple, burgundy, and eggplant, for example. And depending on what colors and patterns it's combined with, it can turn distinctly playful, feminine, or masculine. As white is added, and it becomes more enriched with light, it takes on a less formal mood.

Bringing Violet Into the Scene

If you're venturing into the world of violet for the first time, intrigued at its potential to define a mood or to just break up a monotonous palette, tread lightly. For example, if you have a sleek, contemporary couch in either white, brown, black, or gold, add violet in richly patterned or solid dark brown pillows, or throws. Or, take that tiny powder room and paint it the darkest violet you can find. Accent it with a collection of gold-framed mirrors to create a regal room, or silver-framed pictures to support a clean contemporary theme. You might also try choosing a wallpaper pattern in which violet takes the lead in that powder room, and

accent the paper with purple towels and rugs. This way, you won't be making a huge violet commitment, but you'll have freshened your palette and upped your interest level. If, on the other hand, you're ready to take a bigger violet step, consider using it in a room you can accessorize with colors you do normally relate to and can integrate easily—perhaps in your bedroom, dining room, or in its deepest shade, a study or den. Pastels work nicely in the bedroom— pale violet, pink, yellow, and green, for example. In more public rooms, deeper shades might be the best choice.

Violet Combinations

When you combine violet with other colors, you can create an interesting and unusual palette because it is a color with a high surprise factor, and that alone can make it fun to work with. Some combinations to consider follow. And remember, from dark to light versions, these combinations are distinct and compelling:

• violet and gold
• violet and lime
• violet and tomato red
• violet and gray
• violet and apple green and gold

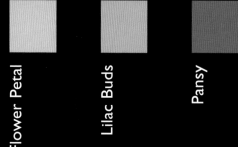

Majestic

Royal

Fantasy

Bridal Hue

Flower Petal

Lilac Buds

Pansy

Lilac walls and a little purple chair accent give this sitting room a unique flavor. Use a combination like this on a smaller scale just as successfully. Try lilac walls in your dressing room or bath, and accent with wallpaper that has a purple theme. Accessorize with burgundy, deep purple, and lilac with a floral scatter rug, towels, and glass soapdish or vase.

Purple, blue, and lilac take what could have been a small, boring, square dining area, and transform it into a striking space where color reigns.

MICHELLE LAMB, A COLOR TREND WATCHER BASED IN MINNESOTA:

"No one has ever asked me my favorite color!... I am pleased to tell you it's purple, and it's been that since the twelfth grade. In the past I have liked it against stark white; today I like it with pinks, greens, and particularly against a green-cast yellow called natural cane. I also like purple that is influenced by brown. In my color forecast I call it plum—brown, and it's an awfully exotic color."

NORTH CAROLINA ARCHITECT SARAH SUSANKA:

"I've gone through phases. I had the phase of rust reds and reddish tones, then greens. Now I'm now in my purple phase, and mauves, with a little red rust. And I'm wearing purple too! I recently bought a dark blue couch and chairs, and it goes well with my rug that has blue, green, mauve, and purples in it."

THOMAS JAYNE, A NEW YORK–BASED INTERIOR DESIGNER:

"I think purple is hard to use, and it may be because of the religious overtones, or because it looks like bad satin lingerie."

NEW YORK INTERIOR DESIGNER
JAMES RIXNER:

"Lilac always reminds me of spring and a refreshing renewal of the spirit. I use this color when I'm conveying a youthful, fresh feeling. It has a positive energy that plays well with many other colors."

CHRIS CASSON MADDEN, DESIGN EXPERT,
AUTHOR, FURNITURE DESIGNER:

"Lavender is the new color, and if you want to be au courant, [toss] a lavender throw into a room or a plumb leather chair or chaise, or pillows. I don't think home design is about trend[s] but a lot of people like to spark up a room, and bring in the color for the season."

MARY DOUGLAS DRYSDALE,
A WASHINGTON, D.C.–BASED
INTERIOR DESIGNER:

"Get some foam core and experiment with paint. Discover what you like. Pick a color family and play. See what you respond to, and then ask yourself 'what is this color doing for me. Does it make me feel like I'm in the country, sophisticated, etc.?' Then go a step beyond and create your own palette."

Most people would be hard-pressed to imagine a purple living room, but as demonstrated here, going monochromatic can work quite well, producing a soft, peaceful place.

Pale violet walls framed in white is
an unexpected combination for a dining
room, but it works quite well to create
a pleasant space. Introducing rose and
lilac at the table support the springlike palette.

Icy

Pure and elemental, an icy palette is modern and clean. Like the first gust of winter, even the softest cool violet palette is a bracing reminder of the color of sunlight as it plays upon ice and snow. At its deepest saturation, blue-violet is boldly expressive, becoming mysteriously inviting when small doses of black are added to its intense indigo hues. Mix this glacial color with shiny chrome and glass accents, and add steely dark grays for a contemporary feel. Combine with red-based purples and magenta for a warm yet still modern mood.

Balance the crispness of an icy color scheme with natural background hues like oatmeal, buff, and ecru. Add the smallest touches of aquamarine and chartreuse to uplift and energize any blue-violet scheme.

Cool violet is a Spartan hue that reflects holistic living and inspires meditative decor. Use pastel tints of this elemental hue to showcase austere spaces. Redefine the infamous great room popularized in the 1970s with an arctic color palette. Translucent fabrics, synthetics, and plastics fuse with concrete and polished pine for a look that will be tomorrow's classic. Select an eclectic mix of vintage finds and futuristic furnishings, such as angular furniture of metal and wood, fabrics that feature geometric patterns, and spherical lighting. Modular Scandinavian and Danish furnishings give an icy interior its edge—look for shelves that double as room dividers, linear storage units, and free-floating platform beds.

[ABOVE]
Mix soft gray blue with silver and marble decorative accents to create a bath with a cool, tranquil atmosphere.

[RIGHT]
Use the palest icy blue to outline and emphasize architectural features, such as this stairway and rails. The warm tones of a chocolate brown carpet and an antique fruitwood side chair, the perfect complements to a cool blue palette, soften the Spartan lines of the space.

104
102
100

101
105
107

105
103
100

107
106
108

108
107
106

110
107
105

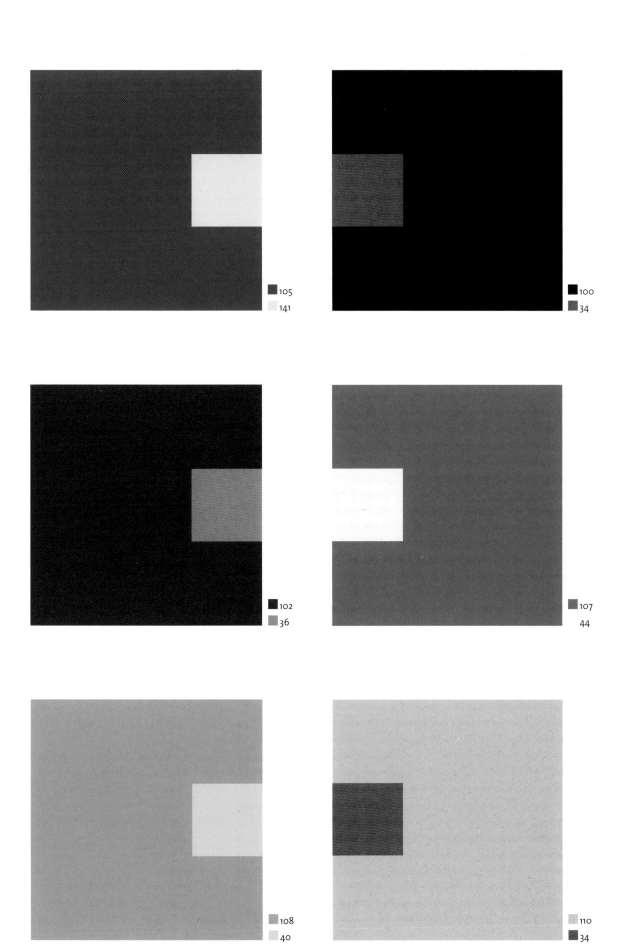

105
141

100
34

102
36

107
44

108
40

110
34

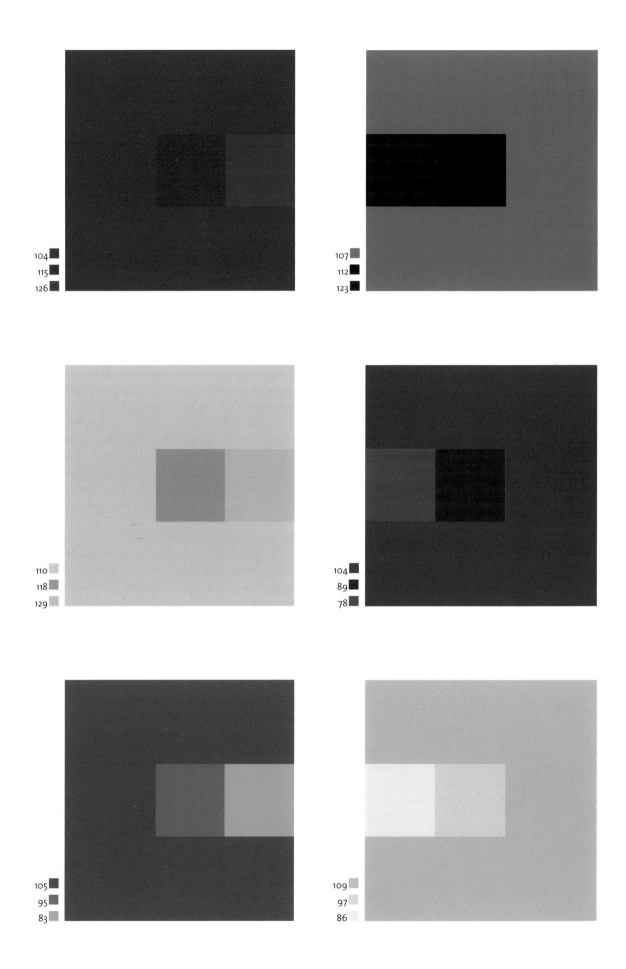

104
115
126

107
112
123

110
118
129

104
89
78

105
95
83

109
97
86

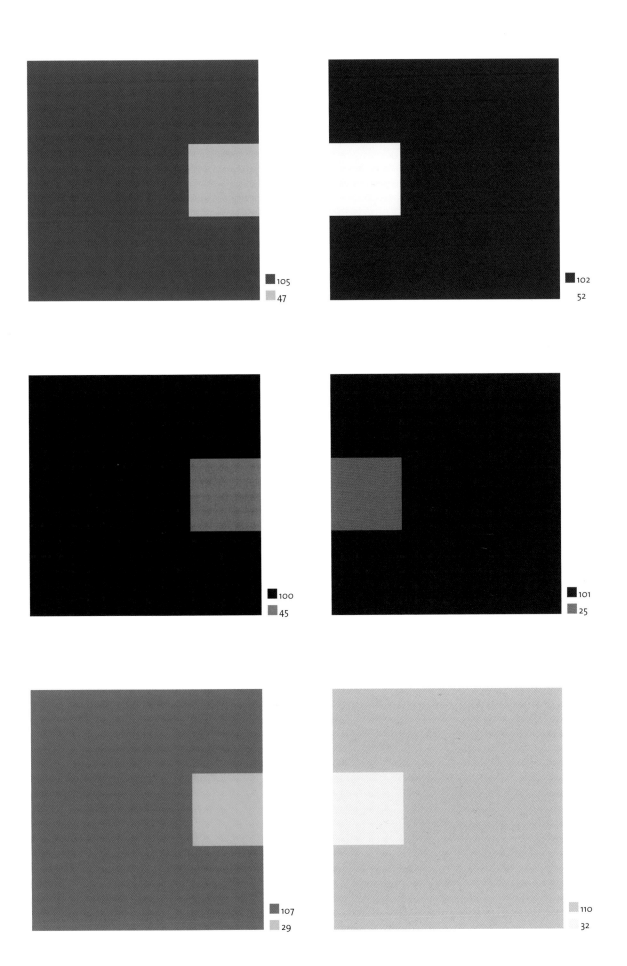

105
47

102
52

100
45

101
25

107
29

110
32

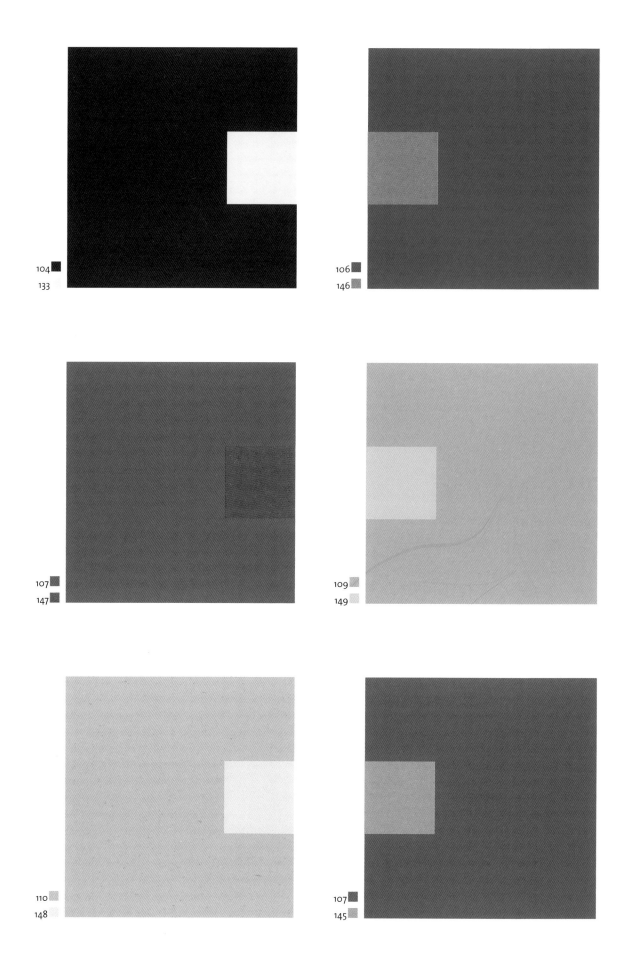

104
133

106
146

107
147

109
149

110
148

107
145

107
142

105
152

100
149

103
142

106
142

100
152

Decorating with
an icy mix

A frosty decor is a balance of clean lines and cooling color delicately weighted to create a soothing, contemplative atmosphere. Icy interior design is both forward-looking and retrospective, featuring sleek mid-century references, such as newly interpreted fabrics and vintage accessories. It's crisp, clean, and glassy, with an ability to work on a large or small scale. Icy hues modernize and are a good choice to revitalize ho-hum spaces, enlivening everything from galley style kitchens to cavernous great rooms.

Natural pines and metals offset this cool blue-violet flooring, furnishings, and accessories in this spacious living area. Linear metal and wood shelving serve as a functional divider in this open-air room.

Icy **Tips**

•Choosing stainless steel surfaces for kitchen appliances instantly gives professional restaurant style to a home kitchen . To refine this crisp, industrial look, consider mounting a backsplash of economical glass (paint the back surface of the glass ice blue after it's cut and beveled to your specifications) or select from a wide array of cooling metal laminates and solid metals designed for vertical surfaces. Metallic surfaces bring a slick modern crispiness to any room especially when variations of blue-violet hues and tints are chosen.

•Modern kitchens are efficient. Glass suspension shelves that secure with cables create parallel storage that's instantly accessible. Hang several rectangular or corner shelves to keep cooking staples at your fingertips. Use sleek metal or glass countertop containers for items you cook with daily. Plan specialized work zones for favorite activities like baking by grouping mixing bowls, pastry bags, measuring cups and spoons in one area of the kitchen.

•Cultivate an icy scheme by displaying blue-violet irises and hyacinths in clear glass containers. Plant four to six bulbs in a 4-inch plastic pot; once shoots are established and reach 3-4 inches, wash the potting soil off of the roots and replant in parfait glasses or recycled jars for a dramatic view of blooms and tangled, exposed roots.

•Combine icy blue-violet colors with the classic clean lines of furnishings designed by mid-century modernists. These design classics will never go out of fashion. Invest in one or two of the "real things" and build a room around a pair of Mies van der Rohe's Barcelona chairs. Keep the mood stark and clean with simple additions, such as a woven hemp rug, a thick glass-topped coffee table, and the clean-lines of a tuxedo couch.

•Use light tints when painting expansive interiors that feature multiple windows. For example, paint the walls of a great room a very light ice blue to create a spacious environment for daily life. Enrich smaller interior spaces like a small foyer or guest bath by painting with a mid-value violet hue.

[ABOVE]
An unusual backsplash of icy blue glazed tiles and the surprise of a deep blue-violet window trim and table top combine to create an eat-in kitchen that's fresh and modern.

[RIGHT]
Keep dark colored walls icy by adding stark white accents. Here, the crisp look of vases and mirrors cools the room and adds dimension and visual interest.

Luxurious

Surround yourself with elements of luxury to transcend everyday life. Pamper yourself and create a decor full of luxury and abundance that speaks to you. A palatial hue, violet moves, sometimes imperceptibly, between warm and cool. Push the limits of monochromatic decorating and combine warm amethyst-red purples with clean, clear violets that have a bluish base. To achieve an almost royal air, blend violet hues with their natural partners, shimmering metallic hues like copper, bronze, and gold. Mix violets with saffron, mulberry, and turquoise for a tapestry of richly hued color. Combine luscious mauves with a variety of greens from sparkling emerald to calming jade. Seek harmonious combinations, such as restful silver gray and pale lilac—they will promote and enhance a lush, meditative mood.

A luxurious interior is the perfect setting for gleaming dark woods, curvilinear furnishings, chaise lounges, corner chairs, and traditional furnishings. In a luxurious environment, much of the decorating fun is to choose pieces that are ever-so-slightly over the top—like a Victorian settee or an ornately carved Middle Eastern chest. Window treatments, a major focal point in any room, can be quite simply grand within a luxurious interior. Be generous with fabric, and then gather, bunch, or swag even simple tab or pencil pleat curtains for an opulent result. Consider the effects of tiebacks, valences, cornice boards, or elegantly scalloped blinds used alone or in tandem with curtains. Invest in a luxurious interior by selecting glamorous fixtures like a crystal chandelier, or embellish with more modest (albeit thoughtful) touches, such as neck rolls positioned at each end of an overstuffed and tufted couch.

[ABOVE]
Pillows, pillows, and more pillows. These plump, plush gold and indigo-hued pillows festooned with tassels, trim, and piping pair well with purply hues.

[RIGHT]
Dress a bed with an abundance of velvety violet. Hang luxuriously exotic candle chandeliers then accent with silky sky blue pillows.

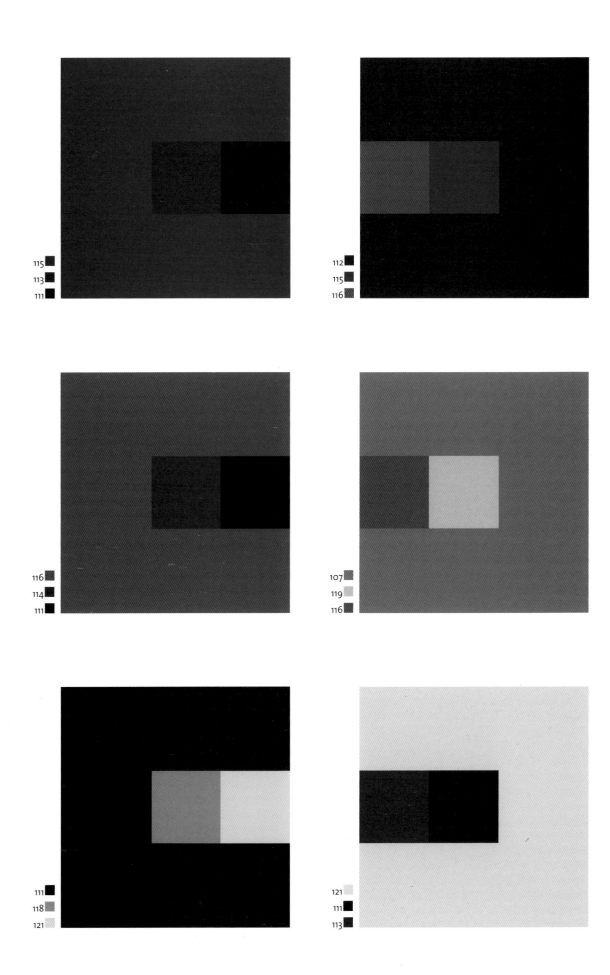

115
113
111

112
115
116

116
114
111

107
119
116

111
118
121

121
111
113

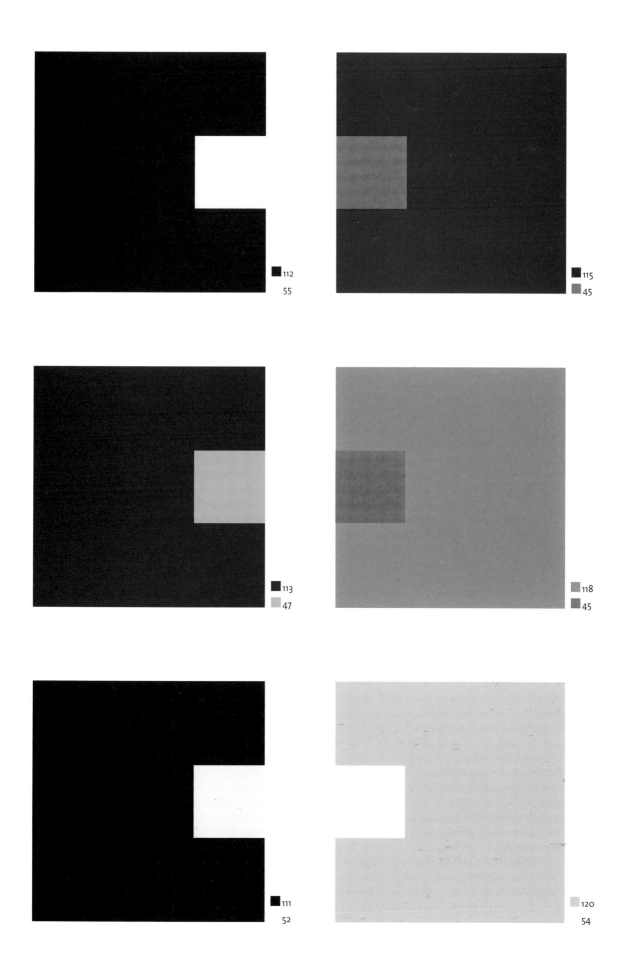

112
55

115
45

113
47

118
45

111
52

120
54

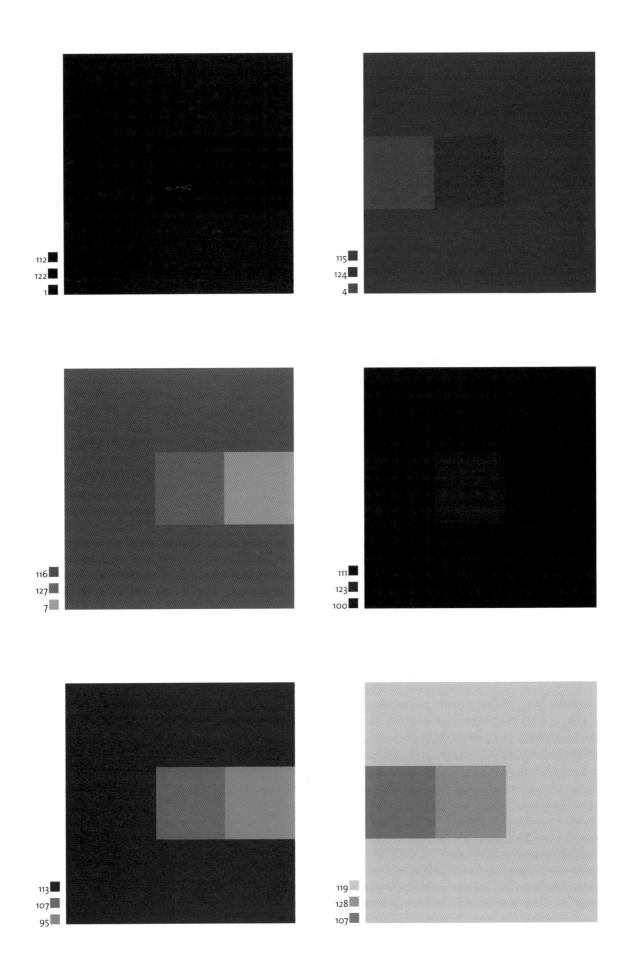

112
122
1

115
124
4

116
127
7

111
123
100

113
107
95

119
128
107

111
34

114
41

116
37

111
64

114
56

121
66

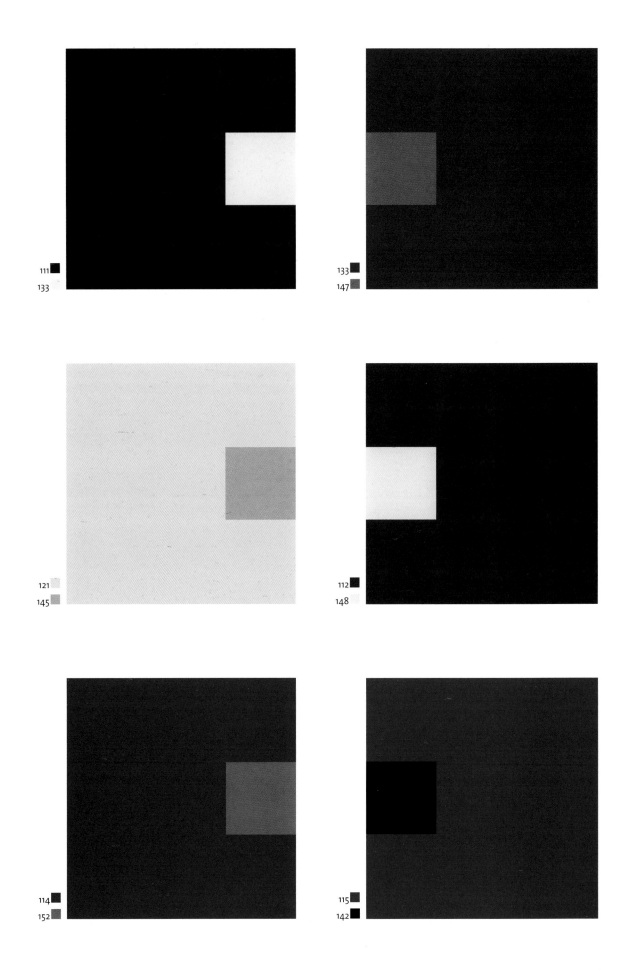

111
133

133
147

121
145

112
148

114
152

115
142

113
149

111
141

116
147

112
151

121
151

121
127

Decorating with a luxurious mix

Vibrant violets were once the exclusive domain of the wealthy and royal. Today, jewel-toned violets abound. Softly tinted, elusive violets are sometimes difficult to capture, much like the subtle shifts and changes of violet rays in natural light. From pale lilac to rich-hued mauve to saturated purples, violet is the color of luxury. Exotic and regal, a violet color scheme can also be fanciful and magical. Violets bring an ethereal mood to just about any environment. Decorate with this luxurious hue and its variations to create an atmosphere of sublime richness.

Sheer drapes in light violet add richness and dimension to this luxurious living room.

Luxurious **Tips**

•Skirted tables bring a lavish, cozy mood to a bedroom or living area. Use fabrics like textured linen, floral chintz, plush velvet, silk damask in plum and mulberry shades, or even animal print fabrics with a sateen finish—top skirted tables with an ample, half-inch-thick glass round.

•Personalize bedding and bath linens with a tone-on-tone monogram, such as violet on a periwinkle terry towel. If you do decide to monogram, invest in good quality linens, but don't feel the need to personalize everything to feel luxurious. Begin with pillowcases and guest towels, building a "monogram wardrobe" over time.

•Employ a butler's table to hold accoutrements so necessary for pampered living. Fill the lift-off tray with necessities for journal writing, such as a leather-bound journal and favorite pen.

•Today bedrooms are often the most luxurious room in a home. Carefully choose from a bevy of headboards and day beds, canopy, and traditional beds. Then dress them up with ruffled pillow shams, comforters, seasonal duvets, and throws.

•A luxurious decor is often the ultimate setting for displaying fascinating objects, such as a collection of silver tipped walking sticks nestled in an umbrella stand. Collectibles, such as antique tea caddies and small English snuff boxes, gain importance when gathered and displayed en masse. The gleam of silver is enhanced when paired with the luxurious hues of palatial violets.

•Distinctive and exotic, the ball and claw foot design of rich mahogany furnishings is particularly stylish and arresting in a luxurious home. Very dark wood finishes, which are often nearly black, accentuate and enrich a violet palette. This quintessential Chippendale motif has Eastern roots. Recall the ancient Chinese icon of the dragon's extended claw reaching for the precious pearl.

[ABOVE]
Combine classic blue with sage greens, purply blues and creamy oatmeal hues to create a decorating mix that's not only historic but refreshingly modern.

[RIGHT]
When decorating for luxury use the soft glow of candles and well placed lamps to assure an illuminated decor that radiates richness.

Romantic

Add romance to your life with old-world charm. Decorate with rosy violet for a romantic decor that's sweetly nostalgic and warm. Use old-fashioned red-violet hues—from pale opalescent shell pink to raspberry red and bejeweled amethyst. Russet browns, nutmeg, and brick shades are natural partners for red-violet hues. Combine these colors for a quaint cottage style. Anchor red-violet with earthbound neutrals like forest green, sand, and stone. Deepen a romantic palette with the addition of raisin and nearly black plum. A romantic scheme can also be wistful—blend palest hues of rose champagne with cream, milk, and biscuit. Accentuate the tender emotions of a romantic decor with touches of primrose yellow and ripe apple green.

A smaller romantic home will favor cottage style, but if your home is spacious, imagine a country manor. Decorate with traditional furnishings that feature rich lustrous woods, antiques or reproductions, and prized heirlooms. Fabrics that are timeworn and true can be used in abundance when evoking a romantic mood. Intersperse everyday fabrics, such as ticking, gingham, and paisley, with fine antique metelasse, heirloom laces, and floral chintz. Hunt for remakes of popular vintage fabrics, particularly from the eras of the 1930s, '40s and '50s. Trims of all kinds are at home in a romantic decor. Look for old-style crocheted trim, crewel work, embroidered designs, ric rac, piping, and scalloped edges to accent soft furnishings, such as bed clothes and drapes.

[ABOVE]
To add instant romance to a room, decorate with the old-fashioned romantic hues of raspberry red and blush pink. Here, a bouquet of flowers on a marble table with a lusterware bowl are displayed as the perfect romantic still-life composition.

[RIGHT]
Anchor a raspberry red living room with furniture in neutral colors, favorite heirlooms, or flea market finds softened by time. Look to rich lustrous wood furnishings or wicker chairs and an old kilim rug for just such accents.

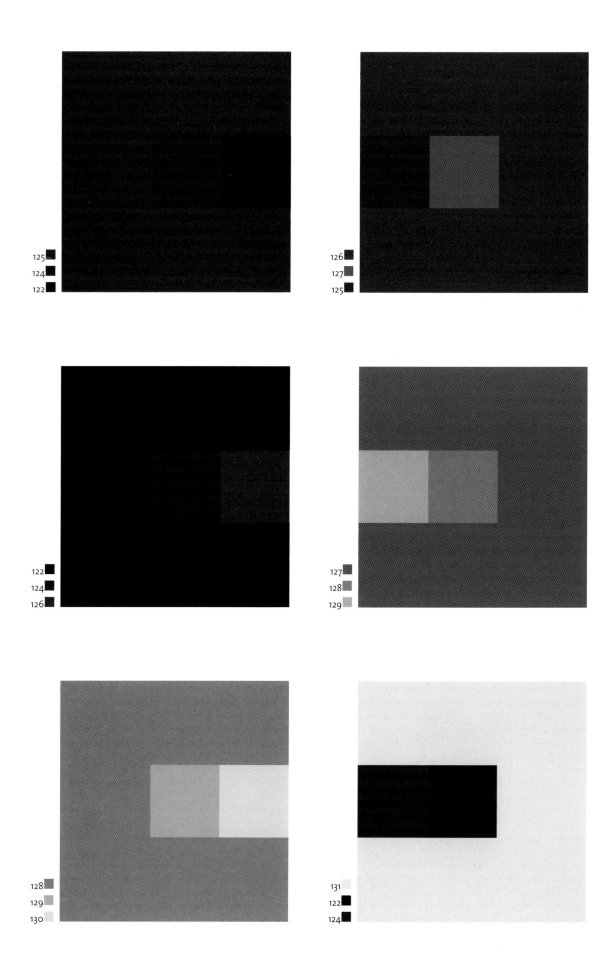

125
124
122

126
127
125

122
124
126

127
128
129

128
129
130

131
122
124

■ 125
□ 64

■ 123
□ 63

■ 122
□ 62

■ 123
■ 57

■ 128
□ 62

□ 131
66

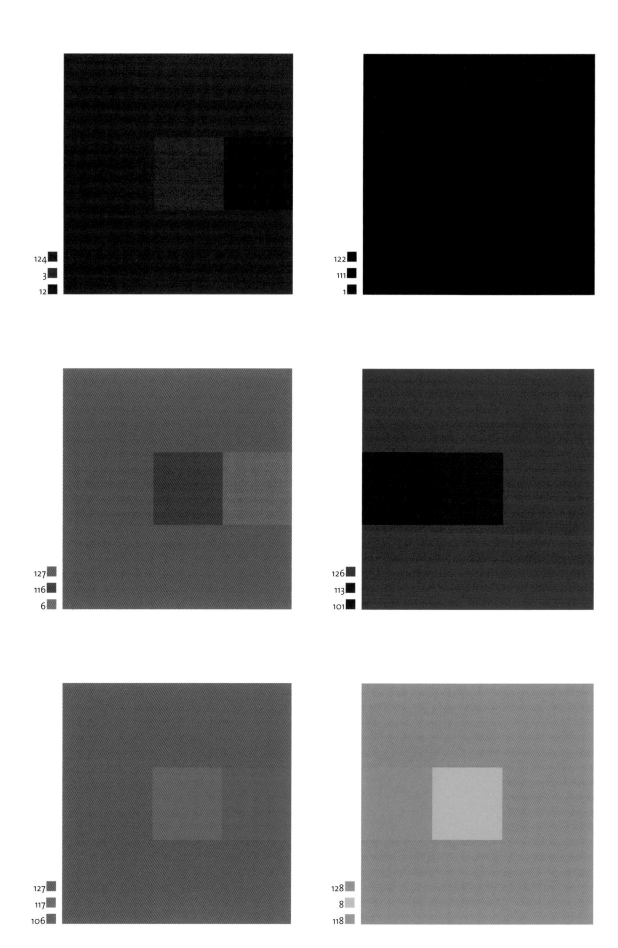

124
3
12

122
111
1

127
116
6

126
113
101

127
117
106

128
8
118

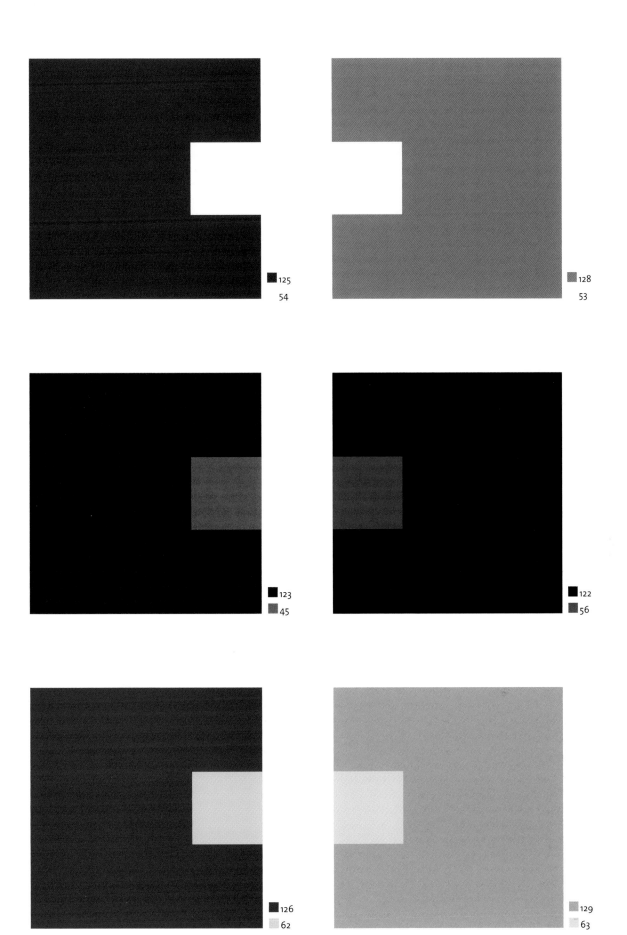

125
54

128
53

123
45

122
56

126
62

129
63

122
147

125
142

123
148

126
145

127
149

129
148

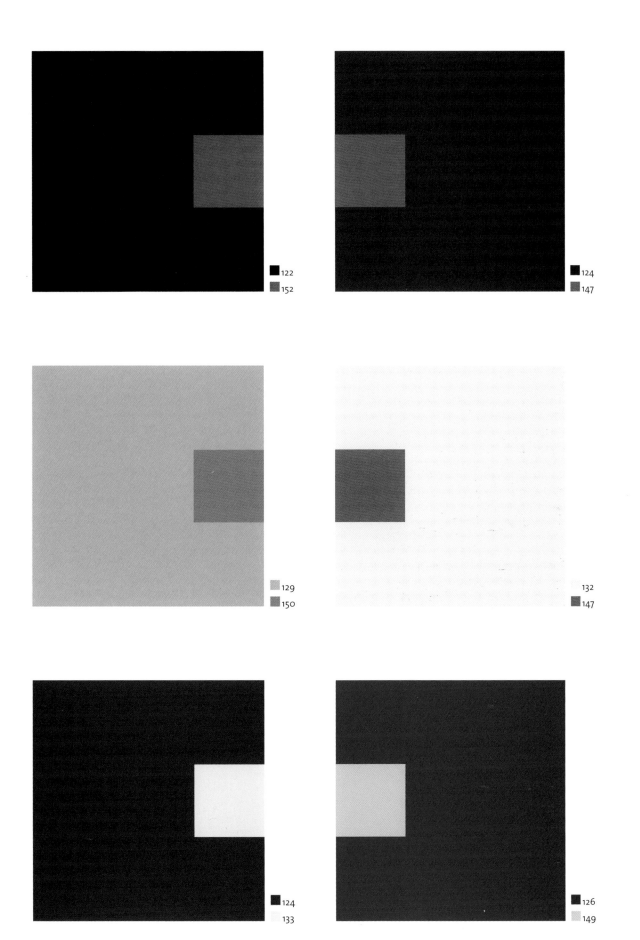

122
152

124
147

129
150

132
147

124
133

126
149

Decorating with
a romantic mix

The key to planning a romantic decor is reach-

ing back into your past. Combine the best of

your old and new worlds for a picturesque style

that will evolve as the years progress. Using a

romantic palette brings a rosy, homespun glow

to decorating. Comfort colors, such as berry reds

and violet burgundy hues, combine effortlessly

with harmonious warm, woodsy hues. Decorate

with antiques as well as hand-me-downs to

achieve a romantic, lived-in mood. A romantic

décor is perfect atmosphere to display a nostal-

gic collection of antique hats, old family photos,

keepsakes, and treasured mementos from

yesteryear as well as today.

Here a tiny alcove is transformed into an intimate and cozy
sleeping space. A skirted round table and slipper chair float in
front of simply swagged window treatments.

Romantic **Tips**

•Don't be afraid to use romantic furnishings that have height and breadth, such as a large armoire. Large-scale furnishings in small rooms often appear charming and quaint. Reconfigure the interior of a large armoire and use it to store fine china, crystal, and table linens in a dining room. Collect china patterns with pastoral scenes depicted in burgundy or violet, and combine with rose-tinted glassware that is finely etched for a colorful, romantic display. Or turn it into a cocktail storage area, well-stocked with bar items and liquors. Position an armoire in your entry as an added coat closet for seasonal winter scarves, coats, gloves, and mittens.

•Honor your family by making an heirloom quilt from keepsake fabrics such as rosy florals, ivory lace, and amethyst velvets. Take a cue from the crazy quilts so popular in Victorian England. Save precious baby clothes, ribbons, favorite clothing, and bits of meaningful fabrics to make your own cherished creation.

•Instantly change the mood of any candlestick chandelier by adding small colonial lampshades, widely available in a variety of colors and patterns. Choose deep purples or black with gilt trim; for cooler months, switch to tiny floral patterns on cream to greet spring.

•Bring the romance of an old hotel to your bath. Select oversized porcelain pedestal sinks and toilets, change fittings and faucets to a soft pewter or gleaming chrome finish, and install reproductions of 1920s-style light fixtures. Finally, stock with stacks of fluffy white quality towels, luxury soaps, and crisp cotton linens.

[ABOVE]
These toile de Jouy pillows feature illustrations of pastoral scenes in rosy pink and rich berry hues, a fitting accent for any romantic room.

[RIGHT]
A mirrored coat-closet door creates the illusion of space in this small foyer by reflecting toile de Jouy wallpaper and drapes within this picturesque entry to a sitting room.

Use white and brown to complement art
objects that share a view. You wouldn't
notice the lines on the vase, or the exquisite muscles on the cougar, if color
backed these objects. Also, having the
brown precede the white in these rooms
provides the perfect visual frame for
what's to come.

Neutrals are a major part of Mother Earth's base palette and are therefore both familiar and comforting. Think about the neutral tones we see everyday—sand and soil, variegated soft tones on seashells and stone. In bringing these colors into our homes, we can complement the tones and textures of natural fibers, wood hues, and shapes. In addition, neutrals frame and extend your outside views like no color can.

The all-white or champagne-colored room (walls and furnishings) lets the shape of the furnishings, whether they are ultra-sleek or down-filled and cushy, shine through. The same holds true for a black marble sculpture, or a simple wrought-iron umbrella stand set against a neutral wall. You are not caught up in seeing how color plays off them; rather you embrace the art of the piece.

But, as many designers say, choosing colors is quite personal—it's your point of view and what makes you happy that matters.

Taupe · Gray · Parchment · Gunmetal · Black · Khaki · Brown

There is something totally serene about an all-white room. You notice the details and shapes you might have overlooked in a room doused in color. In addition, everything has equal importance in the view. When color comes in via a little plant, bowl of apples, or glass, it becomes more art than reality. If you have the slightest curiosity about what you could create with white, but feel a big room is too daring, try it out in an entryway or small guest bedroom.

KELLY HOPPEN,
A LONDON-BASED INTERIOR DESIGNER:

"I have spent many hours mixing colors because I could never find the perfect paint. The first collection that I brought out was called 'The Perfect Neutrals'... I discovered that it was not only my belief and passion that neutrals work best as a backdrop for our environ-ments. If you use them as a base, anything you put with it works and one never really tires of it."

MINNESOTA-BASED COLORIST,
SUSAN MOORE:

"I like combinations of color; it's all about what they do to each other. My living room is palomino pony (a sand color) and saddle on the ceiling and the woodwork is dark. My dining room is deep red with a saffron ceiling so color bounces all over. And my kitchen is a greenish yellow with a gold ceiling. Everywhere you look you see color!"

JOE RUGGERIO, HOST AND PRODUCER OF HGTV'S *HOME DESIGN* SERIES:

"I like all color. But if I had to pick, I'd look toward my office. It's a sandy, non-color, something you can accent."

RHODE ISLAND–BASED ARCHITECT

DAVID ANDREOZZI:

"The use of neutrals in architecture, to me, relates a structure to Mother Earth...a red cedar-shingled New England barn, a white cedar-shingled Nantucket boathouse, and a Georgetown brick home have one thing in common...their individual vernacular relationship to their surroundings. To the end ...neutrals provide the base this connection."

LONDON ARCHITECT

ARTHUR COLLIN:

"All-white interiors are a contemporary cliché. In practice there is no such thing as a standard white and any particular white is not necessarily the same as any other white. Our project for a 'white apartment' in London (shown in London Rooms) embraces the subtle differences that plague color matching by adopting a color scheme using three very subtly different whites. The differences between these whites achieves a subtle decorative effect that results in a warmth quite different to clichéd white minimalism."

There is a lot to see and study in this elegant room—beautiful, rich fabric on the couch and chair, sculpture, and paintings. Using a toned-down palette for all of these things, including the wall, makes for a visually rich, engaging space.

Greenish-gray, beige, brown, and honey
make up the palette of this Zen-like living room and dining area. Keeping the
neutrals as the anchor lets the interesting dark and lightwoods stand out like
free-floating sculptures.

In this big open family living space, the decision to use pale pastel paint and neutral furnishings and carpets works well by allowing the eye to fully appreciate the beautiful craftsmanship of the woodwork, architecture, and in the case of the living room, take in the outside views.

Gunmetal-gray might not be the first color to come to mind for a bedroom, but it works to create a cozy space with a sense of neutrality that is calming and peaceful.

JEFFREY BILHUBER,

AN INTERIOR DESIGNER IN NEW YORK:

"Obsidian! It's the color of a match strike, a graphite color; it's a brown-based black and has the deepest body and most life of any supersaturated color I know of. And whites. I just painted all my doors—all 11.5 feet high—three shades of white: linen, bone, and off-white from the Benjamin Moore Cameo collection. It adds more dimension to the woodwork—depth and detail that is lacking in stingy twentieth-century construction."

ERIC COHLER,

AN INTERIOR DESIGNER IN NEW YORK:

"In fabrics I tend to favor neutrals and earth tones; for contrast I play with texture and fabric weight rather than color. I am also addicted to art and sculpture and take many fabric cues from a client's collection. The richer the collection of art, the simpler the background."

CELESTE COOPER, AN INTERIOR DESIGNER IN NEW YORK AND BOSTON:

"I often use strong color in a foyer or a powder room, rooms one does not spend a lot of time in, rooms that one moves through and does not linger. I use it for drama, for the sense of the unexpected (the accepted theory is to paint small rooms light colors to make them seem bigger, which is a fallacy), and for how it fools the eye... when you walk into a neutral room after passing through a foyer painted a deep color the room appears even larger."

LINDA CHASE,
AN INTERIOR DESIGNER IN CONNECTICUT:

"I love color, especially the jewel tones. I've done projects with creams and off-whites, but my personal opinion is I don't think anything can impact space as quickly and with more impact than color, and I don't think there's anything that has more psychological impact on space than color."

PARIS DESIGNER
SYLVIE NEGRE:

"In the south of France, Corsica, for example, along the Mediterranean Sea where the sun is very bright, I will often choose very simple, light colors. A shade of beige on the floor, white or sand color on the walls, and doors in oak..."

Sometimes the simplest palette makes for the most elegant. Here a milky-white room gets punched up with midnight black and gold via a pillow, lamp, and lacquer box. This is a great color combo for small and large spaces, and is both classy and classic.

The all-natural textures of wood, glass, silver, and even seashells warm up a casual all-white room. Remember, white gives you a unique decorating freedom, a canvas of sorts, where collections of old and new objects and oddities can stand on the same plane.

White and gold in this bedroom provide a clean, crisp environment to show off the interesting shape of this room, architectural details, and the beautiful warmth of the hardwood floor. If you have interesting architectural details in your home, think about painting them with gold.

The focal points in this dining room are the scroll-backed, neutral-striped chairs all hugging the rich woodsy table. Your eye floats to the back of the room to the view, with no bright color to disrupt your trip. When you're designing your rooms, think about the view you want to create.

RON FLEEGER, OF FLEEGER INC., NEW YORK, PRESIDENT AND CREATIVE DIRECTOR, INTERIOR DESIGN, ARCHITECTURAL DESIGN, HOME FURNISHINGS DESIGN:

"I love neutrals. Neutrals doesn't mean boring. They provide a great place for people—inviting and cozy without knocking the hell out of them. Neutrals don't overpower people's personalities. When I think of space I think of people in there."

MICHAEL SCANLON, AN INTERIOR DESIGNER IN BOSTON:

"The most aggressive color we have is dead white. It jumps right out in your face because the walls reflect every bit of light that hits them."

HALIMA TAHA, AMERICAN AND AFRICAN ART EXPERT, AND AUTHOR:

"I love white walls because the absence of color allows me to experience the color that's here in the artwork. I allow white to create distance between art and the room, so the art seems to be hanging out..."

RHODE ISLAND ARCHITECT

DAVID ANDREOZZI:

"Color, like finish landscaping, is the one of the most ignored design elements in architecture today. Most architectural schools dismiss color as being secondary to the design... when in fact... most of the great architecture that provides the datum from which we as architects learn, use color and materials as in integral part of the design. When did this division in occur? It is tragic."

BOSTON-BASED INTERIOR DESIGNER

MICHAEL SCANLON:

"My approach to color comes from my experience as a painter. You discover when you're constructing on canvas that colors define distance. There's a technical term called aerial perspective, which deals with the way colors recede or come forward so when I approach applying color, the question is where do I want to place objects in space. I have a concept of the color wheel that is three dimensional. If you train yourself to think this way, you will be surprised by what you discover."

Another pleasant aspect of neutrals is that they stand quietly in the background, allowing the palette and textures of fabric and furnishings to shine through. The key is choosing the right neutral to let the best attributes of what you have take the spotlight. This is a perfect example; your eye takes in everything from the painting to the chair.

Cinnamon and toasted-brown partner well
in this elegant living room. It is far from
gloomy; in fact it seems to wrap you in
a lush warmth. If this is too much for
you to imagine in your home, consider
a modified version in smaller space
like a study or parlor.

A muted green wall works perfectly to create a clubby-feeling dining room, and allows bright artwork to serve as a welcome beacon.

"Everyone is drawn to different colors. Beige and creams are compromised colors. Continuing to use these means we're lacking expressiveness and joy by becoming the Wonder Bread colors. We're missing self-expression and just plain fun to always go there."

This unusual wall covering with a hint of green gives this bedroom a quiet feeling, and works well to show off the warm and cool palette in the paintings. It also serves as a successful background color for the cluster of pen-and-ink drawings hung in gold and silver frames.

NEW YORK–BASED INTERIOR DESIGNER

ALEXANDRA STODDARD

"To inspire yourself about using color, look at a garden, the sky, or a field."

NEW YORK–BASED INTERIOR DESIGNER

MARRIO BUATTA

"I hate white rooms… It makes me ill to be in them, and reminds me of a hospital."

MINNESOTA-BASED ARCHITECT

KATHERINE HELLBRAND

"I can't disassociate color and texture and composition. So for me, when I isolate color, I can't answer someone or what's best without seeing shapes, shadows, textures, and figures in space. It's very holistic. We may fiddle with one element but it's not possible."

White takes the lead in this pretty dining area, allowing the warm color accents to define the space and the art. Those flaming heads just wouldn't have the same effect if the wall behind were bright yellow.

If you have a decidedly dramatic room, consider what you want to emphasize. Is it the furnishings, architecture, or views? The monochromatic palette makes this two-leveled space look relaxed, elegant, and serene.

mood—with color

A simple black and white color scheme, complete with stainless steel accents, is the perfect way to emphasize a breathtaking urban view.

It is almost second nature for most of us to relate mood and color. We have been trained our entire lives to see the connection—from the time we picked up our first toy fire engine, red said something to us. And so did the pinks and yellows that dressed little girls' dolls. This fashion partnership continues to surface in fashion statements as much as they do in our homes, offices, stores, and even our cars.

Who would argue that black is inappropriate to wear to a formal dinner party, or that a red velvet dress at Christmas is not right? We keep our high-rise offices gray and stiff to keep the mood business-like, and don gray suits to match. And imagine, if you can, how incongruous a pink Mercedes would be!

When it comes to our homes, color matches and combinations are critical to setting the mood and creating a very specific atmosphere. Colors, whether they're in your fabrics, rugs, wall coverings or window treatments all have the power to contribute to a room's mood.

Look through this chapter to see the way color combinations work for you, and with you. And realize that you can set your own stage for drama, romance, and energy by choosing the right mix.

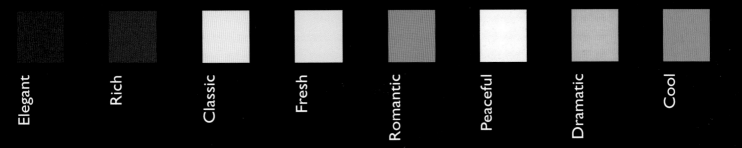

Elegant   Rich   Classic   Fresh   Romantic   Peaceful   Dramatic   Cool

Simple, two-color palettes easily create an elegant mood in a room, as demonstrated by the effective combination of rich cranberry and yellow accents in this bedroom. Imagine how beautiful this room looks when the trees outside the window have turned gold and red with fall, or are topped by creamy snow peaks. Consider how big a role views play in rooms before settling on a palette. You can complement the seasons or match them.

If you're designing a room from scratch think about carrying a color and graphic theme throughout. And don't forget how a bit of whimsy and playfulness can cheer you year round. Here, yellow is the star of the day.

RON FLEEGER, OF FLEEGER INC., NEW YORK, PRESIDENT AND CREATIVE DIRECTOR, INTERIOR DESIGN, ARCHITECTURAL DESIGN, HOME FURNISHINGS DESIGN:

"I think color can affect mood tremendously. If you use blue and white, people think of the sky and water, and it's relaxing. Gray, on the other hand, can suck you of all your energy... Red makes you feel exciting and hot, green makes you think of opulence and the outdoors. Color represents all those things of the life force, and produces different emotions."

KAKI HOCKERSMITH, DESIGNER FOR THE WHITE HOUSE UNDER THE CLINTON ADMINISTRATION:

"I relate color to nature. If you just look outside, nobody is inspired by a gray and dreary day, no flowers in the pots! If you think about why we love the spring and summer, it's because of the flowers, blue sky, and green grass. And if you are comfortable with that, why wouldn't you want that variety and cheerful color palette in your home? You can have those colors you love inside when it's cold and dreary outside!"

**NEW YORK INTERIOR DESIGNER
ALEXANDRA STODDARD:**

"Colors can make you smile. They give you a sense of wonder and hope. They heal, bring joy, and they are there for you like a warm puppy. I'm really concerned that if people can't express themselves with color, how can they express themselves? Why is it we are not able to have that joy—especially with so much sadness in the world?"

**CHRIS CASSON MADDEN: DESIGNER,
AUTHOR, AND HGTV HOST**

"I'm often accused by people of being that lady who always talks about the punch of color! I love to point out the snap or punch of color though because color does bring a room to life. I'm sitting here right now in my little study and I have an old gilt mirror with a band of velvet, red ribbon around my Shaker boxes, and my raspberry red plaid chaise nearby... Diana Vreeland would be happy and proud to see me!"

**NEW YORK BASED INTERIOR DESIGNER
ERIC COHLER:**

"Color, for me, sets the mood of my rooms and gives a heightened sense of scale and drama. I find that darker colors make walls recede and actually seem larger—rather than the reverse. Above all I like harmony in my colors."

When you're choosing wall colors and fabrics, you need to balance your love of a hue with the mood you're trying to achieve. Here, a dramatic and elegant space is also quiet and soothing with the mint green walls and peach fabric.

Choose your favorite color and bathe a
room in versions of it. Yellow, gold, and
touches of burnt orange with period furnishings create an Old World elegance in
this dining area.

When your ceiling looks like the facets
of a highly polished diamond, there's
really no need to detract with lots of
objects d'art. This all-white bed floats like
a giant cloud in this sensual sleep space.

This designer created a dining area that is relaxing and engaging. There's lots of texture and a variety of shapes that soothe and capture your eye. The minimal amount of color works well, giving the spotlight to art.

NEW YORK–BASED AUTHOR, LECTURER, BENJAMIN MOORE ARCHIVE CONSULTANT BARBARA MAYER:

"I think personal taste is more important than research findings on what color does to mood."

TINA SUTTON, FASHION AND COLOR CONSULTANT, BOSTON:

"Color can create moods by emotionally connecting with people. So ideally pick colors that are personal favorites for private rooms, like bedrooms or home offices, while public rooms, like living rooms and kitchens, do better with colors that have a positive association with the most number of people. Lavenders and purples, for example, are colors many women love many men do not, whereas everyone tends to like the color blue, making it a great choice for living rooms and bathrooms."

KATHERINE HILLBRAND, MINNESOTA-BASED ARCHITECT:

"When we talk about small houses, one trick we have is to start with something simple, and then create contrasts—that makes the space seem bigger. If you walk into a room that is all one palette, it can be extremely soothing, but it can quickly become extremely boring! But if you have a home with a small room that's painted a dark or somber hue, that can be very womb-like and soothing."

MARIO BUATTA,
INTERIOR DESIGNER, NEW YORK:

"You need to have color in your life. It's what makes a dreary apartment happy. For most people though, they've fallen into the white thing, and it's boring! After my clients get over their fear of color, they're happy with the color in their apartments—especially after coming home from a gray city. Color affects your life."

NEW YORK–BASED AUTHOR, LECTURER,
BENJAMIN MOORE ARCHIVE CONSULTANT
BARBARA MAYER:

"I think most people do have an idea of how they want to decorate their room; often they want to emphasize a period—French, Modern, English, Arts and Crafts, and there are certain color choices that were accurate and used in many of these styles. If you want to create a Victorian room, you would be looking at upholstery in deep, rich colors, and walls in deep gold, as well as ruby reds, deep green, and a brilliant deep blue... By the same token, if you love neoclassical, it would be unlikely that you would use those colors. You would be using light, clear colors, like Wedgwood blue, pale green, and white. And there are combinations that can help you create the style you want. If you love the form of neoclassical furnishings, and you don't love the colors that reflect the style, there is nothing wrong with choosing the furniture form and a color scheme you like."

White on white, except for the ebony floor, creates a rather heavenly space and makes for the ultimate serene room. Color seeps in from the views, coloring the walls in different hues as the sun moves across the sky.

u can bring the tropical island mood
side, and hold that relaxed feeling by
mply mimicking the palette in your view!

It's easy to keep the mood formal
and romantic with clean white walls
and period furnishings covered in rich,
subtly colored fabrics.

This city condo's calming color scheme—
a medley of neutrals—works well to
show off an art theme of faces.

**ZINA GLAZEBROOK,
INTERIOR DESIGNER, NEW YORK:**

"Find out what drives you in the room. Is it the fabric, a rug, a piece of glass? Take a look and jump off—take something alarming away from that object."

CELESTE COOPER, INTERIOR DESIGNER, NEW YORK AND BOSTON:

"Sometimes one WANTS to camouflage... flaws in proportions, totally undistinguished architecture, problems in scale. Color can then work to take your mind's eye away from features you don't want to see. And something small in a color will balance something large and neutral."

Here is a bedroom that lifts the spirit. Planted like an indoor flower garden, a pane of glass is the only divider from the natural gardens' smell outside. No matter what the season, you can feel spring and summer's glory.

What else can you say about this room?
It's a natural palette that makes you
smile and feel warm and welcome. It
could work anywhere in your home.

Deep purples and blues with random gold accents, provided for the most part through lighting fixtures, makes this space seem cavernous yet cozy.

NEW YORK–BASED INTERIOR DESIGNER JEFFREY BILHUBER:

"I implore people to paint trim the same all over the house, and change only the wall covers room to room because the trim is the thread that connects all the pieces. If not, you will tumble from room to room as opposed to gliding from room to room."

NEW YORK–BASED INTERIOR DESIGNER LEE BOGART:

"I think years ago we had more stringent rules on color. And today there are no rules. I think you can go by your own gut feeling."

The surprise of lavender on the ceiling punctuates an open, airy bedroom. This technigue works well for rooms with little trim or molding and a modern sensibility.

RQUOISE BLUE GOLD BLACK BLUE GRAY

THE COLOR-CHOICE QUIZ GREEN BEIGE GRAY WHITE

We all want to lead better lives. By incorporating the tenets of this book, you can increase certain positive personality traits by regulating the colors you choose for your interiors. While your color preferences are a definite factor in determining the choice of a room's coloration, with *Color Therapy*, the actual function of the colors takes on greater importance. If there is a color that you prefer to decorate a space with, compare it with the chart to be sure it provides the support your life requires.

Choose the emotional, intellectual, and physical traits that you want to emphasize in the space you are decorating from the grid on pages 138–141. For each room in your home, choose the traits that most relate to your perception of what that room should feel like. For each trait you choose, find the color that imparts that quality on the Color Key, located on page 141. Count up how many times each color is chosen. The total will translate the traits you would like the room to possess into color choices. The largest number will indicate the dominant color in the space; the second highest number will give you the secondary color; and the lowest number will suggest the accent color (see "The Rule of 60-30-10" on page 14). If there is a tie between two colors, choose the color that best serves your needs or that you deem as most appropriate for the space.

For example, you may have totals such as ten blue, six red and four yellow. Your answers could translate to 60 percent blue in the room if you desire stability the most. The secondary color could be red if you wish to increase a sense of family ties, again based on your emotional choices from the grid. Yellow would be your accent color if you want the room to be reflective of high skill. If you are decorating a sun room and you want to impart feelings of warmth, vitality, and freshness to the space, your choices will more than likely relate to verdancy (green) and solar energy (yellow). A third example would be perhaps a bedroom in which you want feelings of calmness, quietude, and serenity. Remember to decide on the function of the room before choosing your colors.

Sometimes the color combinations can be unexpected, but don't disregard your results out of hand. When the colors you have chosen don't seem to be a good combination, stop focusing on how the colors go together and instead look at the three selections separately. You may realize that you could use a little more of one of the colors in your life, even if it is only the ten percent value. Some colors, such as turquoise or orange, may surprise you. But if you think about it, you may realize that you already use that color in smaller amounts in your home, and the quiz may just reaffirm the colors you have inadvertently chosen in your life.

If there are certain emotional and psychological aspects of your life that you wish to enhance (perhaps you would like to be more outgoing and verbal), choose the emotional traits you desire from the grid and cross-check them against the Color Key. You can then increase the amount of a particular color in your life to promote these traits.

For example, you may want to increase the amount of blue in your life to help you become a more compassionate, caring individual. You can do this in numerous ways: through your interior design, the clothes you wear, or the car you drive. Your exposure to particular colors and their emotional impact should help you to increase these desirable characteristics of your personality. You can use this tactic in the opposite fashion as well, to eliminate traits you find intrusive, such as anger (decrease red, increase blue) or depression (increase yellow, decrease blue). Have fun!

The Color-Choice Chart

ABSOLUTE	ABUNDANCE	ACCOMMODATING	ACCOUNTABLE	ACTIVE	ADORING
AFFECTION	AFFIRMING	AGREEABLE	AIRY	ALERT	ALIVE
ANALYTICAL	ANCIENT	ANIMATED	APPRECIATIVE	ASSURED	ATTENTION-GETTING
ATTRACTIVE	AUGMENTING	AUTHORITY	BINDING	BLENDING	BLESSED
BRACING	BRAVE	BRIGHT	BRILLIANT	CALM	CAPABLE
CAPTIVATING	CAREFUL	CARING	CASUAL	CAUTIONARY	CHALLENGING
CHARISMATIC	CHEERFUL	CLAIRVOYANT	CLARITY	CLEAN	CLOSE
COMFORTABLE	COMMITMENT	COMPASSIONATE	COMPELLING	CONCENTRATION	CONFIDENT
CONSERVATIVE	CONTENTMENT	CORRECT	COURAGEOUS	COZY	CRAFTY
DEDICATED	DEEP FEELINGS	DEFINITE	DELICATE	DEPENDABLE	DESIRE
DIRECT	DIVINE	DREAMY	DRIFTING	DURABLE	DUTIFUL

DYNAMIC	EAGER	EASY	EFFECTIVE	EGO DRIVEN	EMOTIONAL
EMPOWERING	ENCOURAGING	ENTERPRISING	ENTICING	ESTABLISHED	ETERNAL
EXACT	EXPANSIVE	EXPERTISE	FAITHFUL	FAME	FAMILY TIES
FANTASY	FEMININE	FETCHING	FLEXIBLE	FORCEFUL	FORGIVING
FORMAL	FORTHRIGHT	FRESH	FUN	GEMLIKE	GENIAL
GENEROUS	GENIUS	GIVING	GOAL-ORIENTED	GRACIOUS	GROUNDED
HAPPY	HEALING	HEALTHFUL	HEARTY	HEAT	HEAVENLY
HELPFUL	HIGH REGARD	HIGHER POWER	HIGH SKILL	HONESTY	HONOR
HUMBLE	HUMILITY	HUMOROUS	HYPNOTIZING	IDEAL	IMPORTANCE
IMPOSING	IMPRESSIVE	INFINITE	INNER PEACE	INNOCENCE	INSIGHTFUL
INSTRUCTIONAL	INTELLECTUAL	INTERESTING	INTIMATE	INTROSPECTIVE	INTUITIVE

INVENTIVE	KIND	LASTING	LIGHT	LIQUID	LISTENING
LIVELY	LOVE	MAGICAL	MEANINGFUL	MEDITATIVE	MEMORIES
METHODICAL	MODESTY	MYSTERIOUS	NEUTRAL	NEW THOUGHT	NEWNESS
NOBLE	NONCONFORMITY	NONVERBAL	NOURISHING	OPEN	ORDERLY
OUTDOORSY	OUTGOING	PARTICULAR	PASSIONATE	PEACEFUL	PEOPLE-LOVIN
PERCEPTIVE	PERFORMANCE-ENHANCING	PERMANENT	PLAYFUL	PLIABLE	POSITIVE
POTENT	PRECISION	PREPARED	PRESENT TENSE	PRIVATE	PROCEDURAL
PRODUCTIVE	PROFESSIONAL	PROGRESSIVE	PROLIFIC	PROPHETIC	PROSPERITY
PROTEAN	PROTECTING	PROVOCATIVE	PSYCHIC	PURE	QUICK WITTEI
QUIET	RANDOMNESS	RARITY	RATIONAL	REASONING	REASSURING
REENERGIZING	REFLECTIVE	REGAL	REGENERATIVE	RELAXING	RELEASING
RESERVED	RESOLUTE	RESOURCEFUL	RESPONSIBLE	RESTFUL	RESTORATIVE

RESTRAINED	REVERENTIAL	RICH	RISK TAKING	ROBUST	ROYAL
SACRIFICE	SANCTUARY	SATISFACTION	SEARCHING	SECURE	SELF-CONTROL
SELF-ESTEEM	SELFLESS	SENSITIVE	SERENITY	SETTLED	SEXUALITY
SHARING	SHELTERING	SINCERE	SKILLFUL	SNUG	SOFTNESS
SOLID	SOLITUDE	SOOTHING	SPECIFIC	SPIRITUAL	SPONTANEOUS
STABLE	STATELY	STEADFAST	STILLNESS	STRENGTH	STRICT
STRONG WILLED	STURDY	SUBLIME	SUN FILLED	SUPPORTIVE	SURRENDER
SUSTAINING	TALKATIVE	TASTEFUL	TEACHABLE	TEMPORAL	THOUGHTFUL
TOUGH	TRADITION	TRANQUIL	TRANSCENDENT	TRANSPARENT	TRUSTING
TRUST INSPIRING	TRUTHFUL	UNDERSTANDING	UNIFYING	UNIQUE	UNITING
UNIVERSALITY	UNORTHODOX	UNPREDICTABLE	UPLIFTING	VERSATILE	VIBRANT
VISIONARY	VITAL	VULNERABLE	WEALTH	WISDOM	WORSHIPFUL

The Color-Choice Key

Beige	Blending Careful Casual Dutiful	Enterprising Enticing Expansive Flexible	Genial Gracious Hypnotizing Modesty	Neutral New thought Pliable Private	Randomness Sharing Unifying Versatile	
Black	Absolute Authority Calm Correct	Definite Established Faithful Formal	Forthright Infinite Lasting Noble	Orderly Permanent Rational Releasing	Reserved Reverential Specific Tradition	
Blue	Assured Capable Caring Clarity	Compassionate Durable Emotional Giving	Meditative Mysterious Productive Professional	Restful Restrained Sensitive Solid	Stable Steadfast Tasteful Trust inspiring	
Brown	Close Comfortable Contentment Cozy	Deep feelings Easy Encouraging Hearty	Kind Nonverbal Protecting Reassuring	Relaxing Resourceful Restorative Secure	Sheltering Snug Stillness Supportive	
Gold	Binding Brilliant Conservative Desire	Ideal Impressive Intimate Lively	Meaningful Memories Rarity Reflective	Rich Satisfaction Self-esteem Spiritual	Strict Vibrant Wealth Worshipful	
Gray	Accountable Bracing Concentration Dependable	Direct Drifting High regard Imposing	Introspective Resolute Responsible Sanctuary	Settled Skillful Soothing Stately	Strong willed Sturdy Tough Thoughtful	
Green	Abundance Agreeable Alive Animated	Commitment Healing Humility Humorous	Nourishing Outdoorsy Outgoing Prepared	Present tense Prolific Prophetic Prosperity	Quick witted Talkative Teachable	
Orange	Adoring Affirming Alert Appreciative	Cautionary Fame Generous Grounded	Healthful Humble Methodical Provocative	Self-control Selfless Serenity Sincere	Transcendent Truthful Understanding Universality	
Pink	Attractive Expertise Fantasy Feminine	Inventive Love Newness Nonconformity	People loving Playful Precision Quiet	Reenergizing Softness Solitude Tranquil	Unique Unorthodox Unpredictable	
Purple	Compelling Forceful Genius Helpful	Honor Importance Intuitive Magical	Passionate Positive Potent Psychic	Regal Sacrifice Searching Sublime	Uplifting Visionary Wisdom	
Red	Active Analyzing Ancient Brave	Challenging Confident Courageous Dynamic	Effective Ego driven Empowering Family ties	Heat Inner peace Risk taking Robust	Royal Sexuality Uniting	
Turquoise	Augmenting Charismatic Clairvoyant Eager	Eternal Fellowship Fresh Fun	Gem like Insightful Interesting Liquid	Listening Motivational Open	Performance- enhancing Procedural Progressive	Regenerative Vital
White	Accommodating Airy Clean Dedicated	Delicate Dreamy Exact Forgiving	Heavenly Instructional Light Particular	Peaceful Perceptive Protean Pure	Reasoning Surrender Temporal Vulnerable	
Yellow	Attention getting Blessed Bright Captivating	Cheerful Crafty Divine Fetching	Goal-oriented Happy Higher power High skill	Honesty Innocence Intellectual Spontaneous	Strength Sun filled Sustaining Trusting	

Bibliography

Blakemore, Colin, ed. *Vision: Coding and Efficiency*. Cambridge: Cambridge University Press, 1999.

Buckley, Mary, ed. *Color Theory: A Guide to Information Sources*. Detroit: Gale Research Company, 1975.

Davidoff, Jules B. *Cognition Through Color*. Cambridge: MIT Press, 1991.

Gage, John. *Color and Meaning: Art, Science, and Symbolism*. Berkeley: University of California Press, 1999.

Garau, Augusto. *Color Harmonies*. Translated by Nicola Bruno. Chicago: University of Chicago Press, 1993.

Gerritsen, Franz. *Theory and Practice of Color: A Color Theory Based on Laws of Perception*. New York: Van Nostrand Reinhold, 1975.

Lüscher, Max. *The Lüscher Color Test*. Translated from the German and edited by Ian A. Scott. New York: Random House, 1969.

Miller, David. *The Wisdom of the Eye*. San Diego: Academic Press, 2000.

Riley, Charles A. *Color Codes: Modern Theories of Color in Philosophy, Painting and Architecture, Literature, Music, and Psychology*. Hanover: University Press of New England, 1995.

Rodiek, Robert W. *The First Steps in Seeing*. Sunderland: Sinauer and Associates, 1998.

Sheppard, Joseph. *Human Color Perception: A Critical Study of the Experimental Foundation*. New York: American Elsevier Publishing Company, 1968.

Teevan, Richard Collier, and Birney, Robert C., eds. *Color Vision: An Enduring Problem in Psychology*. Princeton: Van Nostrand Reinhold, 1961.

directory of photographers and designers

Abode UK, 37; 139; 147; 179; 180; 213; 245

Artville Stock, 17

Courtesy of Laura Ashley, 190; 202; 234; 244

Gordon Beall/Drysdale, Inc., 73; 281; 283

Grey Crawford/www.beateworks.com, 157

Tim Street-Porter/www.beateworks.com, 97; 219; 223

Antoine Bootz, 71; 72; 95; 98; 105; 156

Antoine Bootz/Drysdale, Inc., 150

Jaime Ardiles-Arce/Bromley-Caldari Architects, 292

Richard Barnes/Bromley-Caldari Architects, 278

Kelly Bugden/Ned Marshall, Inc., 70

Kelly Bugden/Eric Cohler, Inc., 264; 274; 275

Jonn Coolidge, 12; 26; 49

Courtesy of Crate & Barrel, 96; 118; 119; 159; 199

Glenn Daidone, Boston/Denny Duffy Design, 285; 289

Derrick & Love/Fraser Associates, 69

Phillip Ennis/Samuel Botero & Associates, 85

Phillip Ennis/Christopher Coleman Interior Design, 154

Phillip Ennis/Charles Riley, Design, 116

Luca Trovato/Lucretia Moroni/Fatto A Mano Ltd., 48

Stuart O'Sullivan/Faulding Architecture & Design, Inc., 214

Susumu Sato/Faulding Architecture & Design, Inc., 188

Andrew Garn/Thomas Jayne Studio, Inc., 132

Elizabeth Glasgow/Zina Glazebrook, ZG Design, 262; 263; 284; 290; 291

Courtesy of The Glidden Company, 87; 169; 181

Jon Heil/Christopher Coleman Interior Design, 68

Courtesy of Ikea, 106; 115

Simon Brown/The Interior Archive/Rebecca Hossack, Artist, 75

Tim Clinch/The Interior Archive/Nacho James Design, 83

Jacques Dirand/The Interior Archive/Michel Klein Design, 74

Fritz von der Schulenburg/The Interior Archive; 61; 255

Fritz von der Schulenburg/The Interior Archive/
    Andrea de Montal Design, 212

Fritz von der Schulenburg/The Interior Archive/
    Property: Franshoek, 211

Fritz von der Schulenburg/The Interior Archive/
    Peter Hoffa & Serge Kobin Design, 117

Fritz von der Schulenburg/The Interior Archive/
    Nico Rensch Design, 128; 231

Henry Wilson/The Interior Archive, 84; 167; 185; 187

Henry Wilson/The Interior Archive/Andrea de Montal Design, 256

Henry Wilson/The Interior Archive/Christopher Moore Design, 257

Wulf Bradrock/Jahreszeiten Verlag, 25; 50; 51

Hayo Heye/Jahreszeiten Verlag, 39

Barbel Miebach/Jahreszeiten Verlag, 16; 28

Architektur und Wohnen/Heiner Orth/Jahreszeiten Verlag, 19; 20; 21; 36

Sven C. Raben/Jahreszeiten Verlag, 11

Christi Roehl/Jahreszeiten Verlag, 54

St. Christiansen/Jahreszeiten Verlag, 52

Jeanette Schaun/Jahreszeiten Verlag, 53

Helge Tundt/Jahreszeiten Verlag, 34

Kit Latham/Thomas Jayne Studio, Inc., 133 (bottom)

Andrew Lautman/Drysdale, Inc., 102

Tim Lee/Anthony Antine, Antine Shin, LLC, 273

Living Etc./IPC Syndication, 27

Steve Dalton/Living Etc./IPC Syndication, 13; 30

Jake Fitzjones/Living Etc./IPC Syndication, 41

Winfried Heinze/Living Etc./IPC Syndication, 31; 33

J.P. Masclet/Living Etc./IPC Syndication, 22; 29

Tom Stewart/Living Etc./IPC Syndication, 45

Verity Welstead/Living Etc./IPC Syndication, 14; 42; 46

Peter Margonelli/Linda Chase Associates, Inc., 282

Maura McEvoy/Thomas Jayne Studio, Inc., 103

Maura McEvoy/Thomas Jayne Studio, Inc./
    Courtesy of *Town & Country*, 133 (top); 276

Keith Scott Morton, 59; 158; 170

Michael Paul, 35; 47

Marisa Pelligrini/Anthony Antine, Antine Shin, LLC, 271

Greg Premru, 136; 218; 220; 221; 265; 272

Christopher Drake/Red Cover, 246

Huntley Hedworth/Red Cover, 247

Andreas von Einsiedel/Red Cover, 222; 232; 243

Mark York/Red Cover, 129

Eric Roth, 148; 171

Eric Roth/Greg Cann Design, 182

1999 Life Dream House®, SALA Architects, Inc., 184; 267

©Sargent/Charles Spada Interiors, 155; 186; 287

Durston Saylor/Anthony Antine, Antine Shin, LLC, 280

Stan Schnier/Jennifer Post Design, 137; 258; 268; 269

Courtesy of Spiegel, 235

Tim Street-Porter, 191; 200

Kevin Thomas, 23; 24; 66; 67; 100; 101; 152; 153; 216; 217; 260; 261

Brian Vanden Brink, 130

Dominique Vorillon/Christopher Coleman Interior Design, 64

C.J. Walker/Charles Spada Interiors, 135; 277; 286; 288; 293

Elizabeth Whiting & Associates, 107; 127; 149; 168; 201; 203; 232

about the authors

MARTHA GILL is a freelance designer, author, and teacher at The Portfolio Center in Atlanta, Georgia. She has written numerous books, including several Rockport Publishers' Color Harmony series of guidebooks for selecting natural, jewel, or pastel colors. She is the author, designer, and stylist of the Modern Lifestyle Guides, a collection of books created for people with more style than time. Martha has also consulted on a variety of residential and commercial interiors. She has received national attention for her work, with features in the *Chicago Tribune*, *New York Daily Times*, *Los Angeles Times*, *InStyle* magazine, E's Style network, and appearances on *The View*. She lives with her husband and two children in Atlanta, Georgia.

ANNA KASABIAN has written on numerous topics including living, gardening, dining, traveling, and antiquing in New England, but her great passion is exploring modern interiors and architecturally significant homes, hotels, inns, and gardens. She is the author of *Designing Interiors with Tile: Creative Ideas With Ceramics, Stone, and Mosaic*; *East Coast Rooms*; and *Kids' Rooms* (all by Rockport Publishers). As a contributor to *Cooking Spaces*, she explored the at-home kitchens of some of the most respected chefs and food writers in the United States and abroad. Kasabian's byline regularly appears in *The Boston Globe*, *Boston Magazine*, *New England Travel & Life*, and *Woman's Day*. She also scouts for HGTV, and has appeared on the popular network. She has been featured on National Public Radio's Boston affiliate, WBUR.

MARK MCCAULEY, ASID, is a professional member of the American Society of Interior Designers. He is a former nationally syndicated columnist for the *Chicago Sun-Times* and senior interior designer for Marshall Fields, Chicago. Mr. McCauley is the founder and served as the first editor-in-chief of *Fine Furniture International* Magazine, to which he still contributes regularly. Mr. McCauley has spoken to audiences around the country on interior design philosophy and has made numerous appearances on HGTV. He is currently regional design director for Plunkett's Furniture in Chicago and writes the column "Look Alikes" for the *Chicago Tribune Home and Garden* section. Mr. McCauley resides in the Chicago area with his wife Diana and two sons, Stephan and Christopher. He can be reached by e-mail at ColorTherapy@aol.com.